DATE DUE

NOV 1 6 1999			
JAN 0 3 2000			
ILL RWB 782 916			
4/6/00			
SEP 1 1 2000			
MAY 27 03			
ILL PRC			
2896009			
3/5/04			

DEMCO 38-297

"Mommy, I'm Scared"

· ·

"Mommy, I'm Scared"

*How TV and Movies Frighten Children
and What We Can Do to Protect Them*

Joanne Cantor, Ph.D.

A Harvest Original

Harcourt Brace & Company

San Diego   New York   London

The author gratefully acknowledges the following for permission to include previously published vignettes: Lawrence Erlbaum Associates, Inc. (Mahwah, NJ); J. B. Weaver and R. Tamborini, editors, *Horror Films: Current Research on Audience Preferences and Reactions;* published 1996. Sage Publications, Inc. (Thousand Oaks, CA); Tannis MacBeth Williams, editor, *Tuning In to Young Viewers: Social Science Perspectives on Television;* published 1996. *Trends in Communication* (no. 2), Boom Publishers, The Netherlands (e-mail: Boompubl@euronet.nl).

Library of Congress Cataloging-in-Publication Data
Cantor, Joanne.
Mommy, I'm scared: how TV and movies frighten children and what we can do to protect them/Joanne Cantor.—1st Harvest ed.
p.   cm.
"A Harvest original."
Includes bibliographical references.
ISBN 0-15-100402-1 (hc).—ISBN 0-15-600592-1 (pbk.)
1. Television and children. 2. Motion pictures and children.
3. Fear in children. I. Title.
HQ784.T4C26   1998
302.23′45′083—dc21   98-17080

Text is set in New Baskerville.
Designed by G. B. D. Smith

Printed in the United States of America
A Harvest Original
First edition 1998
F E D C B A

All the personal experiences related in these pages, which have been taken from research my colleagues and I have conducted, from student papers, and from incidents described to me by parents, are real. However, the names of the participants have been changed to protect their privacy.

To my mother,

Elizabeth M. Cantor,

in loving memory

Contents

Preface

Every book author and every publisher struggles to find a title that will communicate what the book is about in a direct and immediate way. The title *Mommy, I'm Scared* was suggested to me by a collaborator early on, and it seems to resonate positively with many people, especially mothers. I chose this title because it's a phrase most mothers have heard, and it's also something most of us have probably uttered to our own mothers. But the title is not intended in any way to exclude the many others to whom children turn when they are frightened—especially not fathers, grandparents, and other caregivers who often play an important, comforting role in the lives of children.

Although this book is based on my own academic research, my primary audience is parents and other people who take care of children. I have therefore tried to write it in a way that these readers would find the most interesting and the most helpful. As a parent myself, I know that

parents want information that will help them understand
their children better and that will give them useful suggestions about how to deal with specific child-rearing problems. In this book, my discussion of children's responses to
frightening mass media is based on the findings of controlled research, but I have also filled these pages with illu-
minating, true examples, many of these presented in a
child's or a parent's own words.

In the interest of this general readership, when I talk
about research, I include only those elements of a study
that will be most useful to people taking care of children.
I am not including the names of my coauthors or other researchers or the dates of publication in the body of the
text and I am not using footnotes, because I felt all these
things might be distracting.

There is a secondary audience for this book, however:
other researchers, medical and mental-health professionals, teachers, college professors, and students—readers
who may well want to know more about the research I'm
describing and may want more concrete documentation
of the arguments I am making. For them, I am including
notes for each chapter at the back of the book. These
notes give the full references for all the studies I am citing
and direct the reader to further sources of information.

"Does Your Mother Know What You Do for a Living?"

"You show *what* to little kids in the name of science?" This
question, in one form or another, has come my way many

times as I make public appearances and discuss my research. And it's a very fair question. Now that I'm a parent
myself, I understand the motivation behind it all the
more. Any discussion of research on children, particularly
when dealing with an emotion as powerful as fright, naturally arouses parental concern. Because much of this book
rests on laboratory research, I would like to clarify exactly
what kind of work I do with children.

One of the themes of this book is that frightening
media depictions can indeed cause long-term damage.
Obviously, it would be extremely unethical to try to
"prove" this harm by exposing children to horrific movies
in the lab and tracking their development over the years.
Although this cannot, should not, and will not be done,
other forms of research go a long way toward demonstrat-
ing that negative effects occur quite often. The evidence I
present for intense emotional disturbances in children
comes from personal accounts by people who have been
exposed to frightening media not in the lab but in their
everyday lives. I base these conclusions on case studies,
retrospective reports, in-depth interviews, and surveys, including those of random samples of parents. Some social
scientists are skeptical of effects that they cannot observe
under strictly controlled conditions. However, when a
child repeatedly wakes up screaming, "The Wicked Witch
of the West is going to get me!" after viewing *The Wizard of
Oz,* who among us would doubt that the movie prompted
these nightmares?

When it comes to studying children's fright reactions in the lab, I, like any social scientist wishing to work with children, must jump a number of official hurdles put up for the child's protection, including obtaining approval by the Human Subjects Committee of my university and gaining the permission of school systems, teachers, parents, and, when appropriate, the children themselves. When requesting parents' permission, we always inform them about the media content their child might see and invite them to preview the program before giving their permission.

The goal in the experimental research we conduct is not to demonstrate harm. Rather, we try to compare the emotional reactions produced by slightly different versions of the same program or by the same program when viewed by different age groups or under different circumstances. For this purpose we need to use only relatively mild stimuli, and we normally expose children to only a brief excerpt of a scary program. We are always careful not to show children material that will be unduly terrifying or more frightening than material available in any number of widely viewed TV shows or movies. Also, we talk about the program with the children after they see it, and they have the opportunity to discuss any lingering fears they might have. To my knowledge, no child has suffered ill effects as a result of participation in this research. Certainly, no child or parent has reported any problems.

How Accurate Are Childhood Memories?

There has been a great deal of controversy among psy-chologists and social scientists over whether childhood memories reported in adulthood are accurate enough to be used as the basis for scientific research. Part of the con-troversy has arisen over news reports that adults have been encouraged or coached to dredge up memories of child-hood abuse—incidents that in many cases may never have happened. Although I base my major conclusions on more well controlled surveys and experiments, I do use adults' reports of their childhood memories when investigating the lingering effects of frightening television and movies.

For those reading this book who may be skeptical, I have a few arguments in defense of the accuracy of the ret-rospective reports included here. Recent research on the validity of childhood memories has concluded that an-swers to questions regarding childhood events tend to be more accurate when people are asked to report on spe-cific events rather than to give a general evaluation of the tenor of their childhood experiences. It has also been found that parents tend to downplay the impact of nega-tive events relative to what their children report.

Several factors increase my trust in these retrospective reports. First, the adults who write these reports achieve no advantage from exaggerating; if anything, reporting on an intense fright response seems to produce embarrassment.

Second, most of these reports contain clear and vivid descriptions of programs and movies, accounts that turn out to be reasonably accurate when compared to the media fare in question. Third, there are great similarities between different adults' independently recalled reactions to the same programs and movies. Fourth, the age trends in these reports are generally consistent with the trends I have observed in controlled studies of immediate or short-term effects.

Finally, although it is possible that the duration of the reported effects may be overstated in some cases (what seemed like a month may have been only a week, for example), the fact that so many adults still report and reveal ongoing emotional disturbances that they trace back to these programs or movies suggests that these events produced extremely intense reactions and that we should not discount the importance of these long-term emotional memories.

—Joanne Cantor, Ph.D.

"Mommy, I'm Scared"

. . . .

Is Your Home Really Your Castle?

. . . .

Confronting the Resident Monster

Remember when your first child was born and you took great pains to childproof your home? You locked away the medications and poisonous cleaning agents, hid the knives and the power tools, put safety covers over the electrical outlets, and maybe placed a gate at the top of the stairs. If you're like many parents, you may even have decorated a room especially for your new baby with cheerful, bright colors and a crib that met the latest safety standards. You probably filled your baby's room with a variety of clean, safe, and adorable toys. When you bought something that your child would see or use, you started thinking about how she would react to it. Your child was going to be brought up in an environment that was not only physically safe but also felt happy and warm and comforting. No one who might harm your child would be invited into your home, and nobody could bring unsafe or inappropriate items to your child without your knowledge or say-so. You were the gatekeeper in charge of your castle—*right?*

Unfortunately, if you are like almost 100 percent of the parents in this country and you have a television, your home is full of uninvited virtual intruders of every stripe— monsters, witches, vicious animals, rapists, child moles- ters, burglars, terrorists, and tornadoes, to name only a few—all ready to disturb that child-friendly environment and pounce on your child's psyche at any moment. If you're concerned about the effect of these images on your child's mental health, you have two choices: Either you get rid of your television or you learn to tame this resident monster.

Chances are, you don't want to get rid of your TV. You probably enjoy watching it yourself and realize that there are many good programs for children. In fact, research now shows that educational television programming viewed at the preschool level can really improve children's chances for success much later in life. Why should you give up on the potential positive effects of television?

This book is for parents who feel that getting rid of their television is not the best option but who want to pro- tect their children from preventable psychological harm. We have come a long way since the fifties, when we had only three channels to choose from and our choices ranged from *Dragnet* to *Hopalong Cassidy* to *The Donna Reed*

Show. Thanks to cable and satellite transmission, we now have 36, 50, even 100 options or more at a time. As a result, today we probably have more television that can inform, entertain, and instruct our children than there was decades ago. At the same time, there is certainly a great deal more television that can unnerve, upset, and traumatize our children than previous generations ever imagined.

Television and movies, by their very nature, have the ability to introduce children to frightening images, events, and ideas, many of which they would not encounter in their entire lives without the mass media. We need to learn how our children are affected by these intruders so we can make better decisions about what they should watch and find ways to help them handle their reactions if they become inordinately troubled.

CHAPTER **ONE**

The Suddenly Crowded Queen-Size Bed

. . . .

A Wake-Up Call to TV and Movie Fright

Every night, in homes all around the country, parents are being confronted by children in distress. Their children are trembling and sobbing or having nightmares or climbing into their parents' bed and refusing to sleep alone. Some of them are suddenly giving up activities that they once enjoyed, feeling anxious about being alone, or refusing to go to new places.

Are these children reacting to the bully who threatened them at school? Are they worried about the child molester who tried to entice them into his car? Are they anxious about the burglar who just broke into their home? Probably not. Most of these children are reacting to something that never even happened to them. They are traumatized by something they saw on television or in a movie. It's as simple as that. What is worse, the anxiety they are experiencing may not go away in days or even weeks. Often it will last months, years, and even longer.

From my fifteen years of research on mass media and children's fears, I am convinced that TV programs and movies are the number one preventable cause of nightmares and anxieties in children. What's more, although many parents are disturbed about the problem, most don't know how to predict what will frighten their child or what to do about it. That is why I've written this book.

That Midnight Visitor

Does the following story sound like something that's happened in *your* home?

Sara was watching *Goosebumps* with her seven-year-old son, Tim, but she was called out of the room when the phone rang. By the time she returned, Tim was staring in horror at gory and grotesque images from an episode of *The X-Files*. In the program, a man had a sore on his stomach, but it wasn't really a sore; it was his twin brother [!], who would growl and be nasty during the day and murder people viciously at night. Sara made Tim turn off the program, but the damage had been done: The whole family had a terrible night. Sara reports that Tim woke up in a fit and admitted that it was the program that had scared him. For a week, he insisted on sleeping in his parents' bed. After that, they made him go to sleep in his own bed, but they'd wake up and find him back in theirs. Sara was

appalled. About a month after the incident, she said Tim
was still scared. He was worried that the vicious creature
could get into their house.

Or maybe this excerpt from a college student's paper
reminds you of something that happened to *you* as a child:

> *I loved every minute of* Poltergeist. *It was like
> nothing I had ever seen. It was gory and scary and so
> exciting. Well, in broad daylight at least. That night at
> home was a completely different story. I was terrified,
> and I didn't know what to do. How could I tell my par-
> ents what I had done and that I was frightened from see-
> ing a movie that they had specifically forbidden me to
> see? But I was in a state of emergency because the clown
> that was now under my bed was about to come out any
> minute if I didn't take immediate action. I built up my
> courage and successfully made it to my parents' room,
> constantly looking over my shoulder. I crawled in be-
> tween my parents in bed, hoping that they wouldn't no-
> tice me, but they did. My mom asked me what was
> wrong, and I mumbled something about the clown and
> the tree outside my window that were trying to take me
> away. (By the way, there are no trees tall enough in New
> York City to reach a window on the seventh floor of an
> apartment building, and I have never even had a clown
> doll.) I'm sure my parents knew what I had done because
> they themselves had seen the movie almost a year earlier.
> I slept with them in their bed for two whole weeks.*

If either of these anecdotes sounds familiar, rest assured that you have a lot of company. Events like these occur all the time, although they don't receive nearly the publicity that other effects of television do.

I started studying children's fright reactions to television and films in the early eighties. At the beginning of my research career, I had looked at some of the more widely studied effects of television, such as how viewing violence makes people more aggressive. But I started thinking about fear effects after several of my graduate students began telling me about their own children's frightened responses to television—reactions they were at a loss to explain. I was reminded of my own experiences as a child. I remember the terror I felt every time I saw the Wicked Witch of the West in *The Wizard of Oz* and how uneasy listening to *Peter and the Wolf* on my record player made me feel. I remember finding it difficult to sleep at night after watching or listening to something scary, but I also remember not wanting to tell my mother about it. I still somehow wanted to see these things, and I certainly didn't want to be told I couldn't watch them—I was the youngest of three children, and, after all, I didn't want to be treated like a baby!

When I began studying children's fright reactions to media, I was mainly interested in them as an academic researcher. Having studied developmental psychology, I was examining how a child's age affects the types of things that will be frightening. I wasn't initially studying long-term effects or the psychological harm caused by media viewing because you can't study these things in controlled laboratory experiments, the method I was trained in. But because I had such vivid memories of my own, and because I was hearing again and again from others who had had similar experiences, I came to the conclusion that studying children's facial expressions as they watched a scary scene or tabulating their ratings of how scared they felt immediately after watching a five-minute film clip was not enough.

So, at the beginning of each semester, I began asking my students to write short papers about anything on television or in a film that had frightened them. I was immediately struck by how deeply disturbed and distressed my students had been by a program or film, and I was amazed by the vividness and emotionality with which they wrote about their experiences. Almost all the students in these classes were able to recall and describe an incident that disturbed them greatly. Only the rare student reported never having been scared. But looking at these papers as a researcher, I still was unsure how widespread these reactions really were. Since students were putting their names on their papers, could some of them have been elaborating their stories to please their professor?

In order to reduce my doubts, I approached the same question differently. I arranged for first-year college students to be offered extra credit for filling out a brief questionnaire. I'll call this the retrospective study. To receive credit they had to answer the following question:

Have you ever been so frightened by a television show or movie that the emotional reaction stayed with you after the program was over?

Their choice was either to say "no," and be done with it, or to say "yes," and describe the experience in a one-page paper followed by a three-page questionnaire. Either response would earn them the same amount of credit. As I saw it, laziness or pressures from course assignments would lead many students to choose the easy "no" response. So I felt more confident that the students who took the trouble to complete the anonymous paper and questionnaire were indeed telling the truth and recounting an incident that had meant a great deal to them.

The response was overwhelming: Out of 103 students who were given this option for receiving extra credit, 96 chose the "yes" response and many of them provided graphic and emotional descriptions of the terror that had been provoked by a movie or TV show. Here are two typical excerpts from their descriptions:

After the movie [Jaws], *I had nightmares for a week straight. Always the same one. I'm in a room filled with water with ducts in the walls. They would suddenly open*

*and dozens of sharks would swim out. I felt trapped with
no place to go. I would usually wake up in a sweat. Oc-
casionally I'll still have that exact same dream. The
movie didn't just affect me at night. To this day I'm
afraid to go into the ocean, sometimes even a lake. I'm
afraid that there will be a shark even if I know deep
down that's impossible.*

    *The movie that I saw that disturbed me very much
was* Friday the Thirteenth, Part 2. *I watched this
movie when I was fourteen years old and it scared me so
much that I couldn't sleep for a whole month. I was scared
of the name Jason and I hated standing under a thatched
roof. At night I needed a night-light so that I could see
everything around me. I was very conscious of the small-
est little noise. I had nightmares about knives, chain saws,
blood, screams, and hockey masks. I was very jumpy.
This kind of slaughter film still has these effects on me.*

These descriptions are very much like the hundreds
of astonishingly intense examples I've collected from students in my classes and other people I have encountered
or who have written to me. One fascinating aspect of the
student papers is how much the students seem to get out
of writing them. The memories of these incidents are
extremely clear, ten and even fifteen years after the fact,
and students find themselves using dramatic and emotional language that they rarely use elsewhere. When stu-

dents talk about these experiences in class discussions, we can often hear the residue of fear in their voices. And although students are sometimes embarrassed to admit how intense and long-lasting their fear reactions were, they are usually quite relieved to learn that so many others in the class have had the same experience. Many students have reported that being encouraged to think about this traumatic incident reignited their fear. But they have often said that writing about it and learning why it may have happened helped them work through some of their anxieties and ended up reducing their fear in the long run.

A Fear That Lingers

Although the question the students answer is about any fear that lasted beyond the time of viewing, these reactions are typically not one-night affairs. In fact, almost two-thirds of the students in the retrospective study reported that their reactions had lasted a week or more. One-fifth of the students said they had not been able to get the movie or program off their mind, and almost half of them said that what they had seen had interfered with their eating or sleeping. You may have noticed that one of the anecdotes includes the phrase "To this day" to describe a movie's lingering effects. This expression is somewhat unusual in ordinary conversation, but as you read on, you will see that it comes up time and again when people talk about their experiences of TV and movie fright. Even though most of these college students were reporting on events that happened to them in their childhood or adolescence, one-fourth of them said that they were still feeling residues of the fear that the program or movie had produced.

Some skeptics might react to all this with a shrug of the shoulders; it is true that some children can see scary movies and not be greatly upset. But this should not lead us to belittle the harm done to millions of others who are more media sensitive.

Obviously, all children are different. One child's thrill is another child's trauma. Many children, even those who suffer afterward, say they enjoy watching scary movies and TV shows. Witness the eternal popularity of horror movies and the current fad in TV shows such as *Are You Afraid of the Dark?* and *Goosebumps*. Many of us like the spine-tingling feeling of being scared as we identify with a TV or movie character who is in danger. This attitude, which I will discuss in more depth in chapter 9, is frequently seen in students' reports.

The real questions are: How much fright can a child take? When does the spine tingling cease to be fun? And when will the fun experienced while viewing come back to haunt a child in the night? And for how long? And how are children, or parents, for that matter, to know before-hand where a child's terror threshold may lie and which program or movie will cross it?

Although fright reactions to television and films have never been in the limelight of public discussion, over the years a number of psychologists and psychiatrists have claimed that these reactions may cause children to be plagued by nightmares, sleep disturbances, and bizarre fantasies. There have been several case studies in medical journals telling about young people who had to be hospitalized for several days or weeks after watching horror movies such as *The Exorcist* and *Invasion of the Body Snatchers*. One recent article reported that two children had suffered from post-traumatic stress disorder, a diagnosis usually reserved for Vietnam War veterans and victims of physical violence, as a result of watching a horror movie on television. One of the children described in the article was hospitalized for eight weeks.

Obviously these are extreme cases. But, I, too, have received reports indicating that medical attention was necessary as a result of viewing a film. Here's one example:

I remember the time ABC broadcast the controversial made-for-television movie The Day After *in 1983. The show terrified me. For several weeks I was absolutely certain there would be a nuclear war. I had literally become obsessed with the concept of worldwide atomic destruction. I was obsessed to the extent where I would actually wake up around 5 A.M. every morning so frightened I would crawl into bed with my parents. I further would not leave my mother's side—not even to go to the bathroom. And I stopped eating. I became very sick after many weeks with this irrational behavior and had to be taken to the doctor.*

This anecdote came from one of the students in the retrospective study. A few years later I met him when he took my course on the effects of the mass media. At that time he told me that he actually had been hospitalized because of his reaction to *The Day After*, but that he had been too embarrassed to admit that fact earlier, even though he knew his paper was anonymous.

Another student cited *Jaws* as the source of her panic attacks. After describing how she quit the swim team in the middle of a race (in a pool, mind you!) the day after seeing the movie, she continued:

> The movie Jaws *affected me in worse ways than a fear for pools. During the summer going into my sophomore year in college, I returned to summer camp after a seven-year hiatus. On the first day, all counselors had to take a swim test in the lake. Needless to say, I refused to get in, failed my test, and haven't gotten in the lake for the past three summers. Every time my campers had swimming, every time I almost got playfully tossed in, and every time I was even near the lake, I would experience small panic-anxiety attacks. I would always have a persistent fear for the water and I could never get too close to the lake. Consequently, these panic-anxiety attacks started to take a toll on my body, eventually wearing me down until I had trouble walking up even the smallest hill. My heart would race uncontrollably fast*

> *and my emotions would change constantly; I was laugh-*
> *ing one moment and crying the next. . . . I don't know*
> *if I have overcome my phobia since I am not around*
> *camp during the year, but because of my panic-anxiety*
> *attacks, I get extremely claustrophobic in elevators.*

Although these last two cases may be exceptional, what I've discovered through my research is that intense and long-lasting media-induced fears are far more common than we think and often linger well into adulthood. There are many, many people who admit, like two of the students already quoted, that they are afraid to swim in oceans or even lakes or pools since watching *Jaws*. Granted, it is not that odd that many people think of that great white shark whenever they swim in the ocean (I know I do!), but when people give up swimming in lakes or pools because they once saw a movie about a shark in the ocean, we should indeed be concerned. For these people, a few hours of entertainment has altered their lives.

Many other people suffer the enduring effects of watching Alfred Hitchcock's *Psycho:*

> *My phobia of taking a shower without anyone in the*
> *house began in October of 1973. . . . No matter how silly*
> *and childish it may seem, five years older and wiser, I*
> *still find myself peering around the shower curtain in*
> *fear of seeing the beholder of my death.*

Jaws and *Psycho* may be the most well-known examples, but there are many, many other shows and movies that have produced effects that won't go away:

> *For years (I'm serious) this movie* [When a Stranger Calls] *has haunted me. For the months following this experience, whenever I was home alone and the phone rang, I feared that the calls were coming from somebody upstairs in my house. A few years ago we moved to a new house where the phones have a panel to show what lines are in use. If I am home alone, I think I subconsciously check to make sure that no other line is being used whenever the phone rings.*

This student's addition of the expression "I'm serious" reflects another interesting aspect of students' papers. The writer seems to be suggesting that the duration of her response is so unreasonable or unusual that I might not believe her. Most of the students who write these papers have no idea how many others have experienced the same effects.

Quite frequently, students talk (sometimes sheepishly) about the elaborate rituals they have developed for coping with their fears. Often these procedures are maintained over long periods of time, sometimes into college. One student reported that she still "protects" herself while sleeping:

When I was around six years old I watched a horror movie about vampires and werewolves preying on innocent people. One behavior that started after this viewing experience is one I still use today. I was convinced vampires would come when I was sleeping, bite my neck, and suck out all my blood. In order to prevent this horrible way of dying, I place a special blanket partially around my neck before I go to sleep. The blanket acts as a barrier between me and the vampire's fangs.

Another student titled her paper "The Bedtime Jump." It began as follows:

To this day, I still leap into my bed from the door after I turn out the light, hoping to avoid any creepy crawly bugs, creatures, or anything else that might run across my feet in the dark. Even though I am almost positive that there really isn't anything on the floor, I do the bedtime jump rather than risk it. I think it all started with the spider movie I watched when I was five or six years old.

And then there's the perennial shower ritual derived from *Psycho*:

For almost two years this had such an impact on me that I would never take a shower unless the curtain was three-fourths open so I could see in the mirror across from

*the shower that no one else was in the bathroom. I even
locked the door at all times. But even that wasn't enough,
so I also pulled out the drawer alongside the door so in
case someone got the door unlocked, they wouldn't be able
to open the door past the drawer.*

Although some of the rituals are almost ludicrous,
some of the recollections are poignant. The following was
the entire description given by one young woman in the
retrospective study, who was told that the expected length
of the paper was about a page:

*The only movie that had any lasting impact causing
me fear was* The Wizard of Oz *when I was little. I used
to sit and cry when the mean witch came on and my parents and older siblings would laugh at me. Then I couldn't
sleep 'cause I thought the witch would come and get me.*

Another description reflects how enduring the impact
was, even though the memory of the movie itself was
vague:

*Although I don't know the name of the film or very
much else about it, I can't get the images to leave my
mind no matter how hard I try.*

Finally, here is an example of a movie that tapped into or
intensified a young man's long-term feelings of paranoia:

Silence of the Lambs has always disturbed me. It's so disturbing because there are people like this out there. They're psychotic and don't care about anything. They like to play with your mind and drive you crazy. Who knows, it may be your best friend. They are out there somewhere, and they may be coming after you or me.

We need to keep in mind here that these are not the reports of psychiatric patients or of young people in trouble. These are university students who, by making it to college, have shown themselves to be relatively successful in their life adjustment. These are not our weakest and most vulnerable young people. And still, something that they never experienced firsthand, but that reached them only via TV or in a movie, has had so profound and distressing an emotional impact. Many of the symptoms they report, such as avoidance of specific activities (especially when there is no rational basis for avoidance), high anxiety levels, recurrent obsessive thoughts, and sleep disturbances, are well-known symptoms of both phobias and post-traumatic stress disorder. Imagine the effects on children who are emotionally at risk!

Spillover Effects

"But he'll get over it," some might say. "A good scare never hurt anyone!" "So what if they worried a bit or had nightmares about a movie? There are lots of things in this world to worry about, so why not this?" As a parent of a young child, I can't really empathize with this attitude. It seems obvious to me that as parents we should want to prevent nightmares and sleep disturbances in our children if we can. And, of course, it's not just emotional distress we need to be concerned with. As some of these examples suggest, the fears induced by media exposure can spill over into everyday life and interfere with otherwise normal activities.

Because I was hearing so many stories of these spillover effects, my colleagues and I designed a study to observe them in a mild form immediately after viewing and to answer a couple of questions: Would watching typical dramatic scenes where people are seriously hurt or die make children worry that they are more likely to become victims of similar accidents? And would seeing scenes like these make children more reluctant to engage in normal activities related to what they had witnessed?

We started with an episode from *Little House on the Prairie*. Although nothing could possibly sound more harmless than the title of this program (which is still on the air in reruns), it was among the top-ten fear-producing shows according to a survey of parents my collaborators and I conducted in the early eighties. Although the series offers a sensitive portrayal of a family facing joys and hardships, it addresses an enormous array of controversial and threatening issues, such as murder, child molestation, and accidental death. The scene we chose was from an episode in which a school for the blind burns down and several people are trapped inside and die in the fire.

We showed the children in our experiment either a five-minute clip from this program or a scene from a movie in which people enjoyed cooking dinner over a campfire without any threat of danger or harm. Still other children saw film clips involving different activities. We then gave the children a questionnaire asking them about a variety of issues. We asked them, for example, how worried they were that various things would happen to them, including being injured in a fire. Lo and behold, those children who had just seen the excerpt from *Little House on the Prairie* were more worried about fires than both the children who saw the other fire scene and children who saw scenes that didn't involve fire at all. What is more telling is that when we later asked them how interested they would be in getting involved in various activities, the kids who had seen *Little House on the Prairie* were less interested than all the others in building a fire in a fireplace. We also found the same type of effect for another movie scene, which showed a drowning. Those children who had just seen that tragic event thought they were more likely to be involved in a dangerous situation in the water, and they were less interested in learning how to paddle a canoe than the other children in the study.

Obviously, what we produced in this controlled experiment was a mild effect that probably did not last very long.

We tried to make sure of this by talking to the children about any continuing fears they might have and using this opportunity to go over guidelines regarding fire and water safety. I think that the minor effect we observed in the lab is in some ways similar to the strong effects I repeatedly see in students' retrospective reports and parents' reports of their children's long-term reactions. For example, one mother I talked to reported that her daughter had learned to ski at the age of four and loved it. However, she abruptly refused to ski anymore after she saw an episode of *Rescue 911* in which a child fell from a chairlift and was shown hanging dangerously by a rope until she was rescued.

Another mother sent me this report:

> *When our youngest daughter was about five, we were traveling in the northwest. One night we watched a James Bond movie on television, containing a scene of a shark that was released into a swimming pool from a grate in the side of the pool. For several days thereafter our daughter refused to go into swimming pools, even at the insistent urging of her older brother and sister. For several years she claimed to be nervous about going into pools where it looked like an underwater shark cage could be hidden.*

The realization that a movie may have interfered with swimming is one of the most common themes in students' papers:

It hadn't occurred to me until just now, but there's probably a connection between having seen and been scared by this movie [Willy Wonka and the Chocolate Factory] *and my extreme fear of having to jump off the diving board at our local YWCA pool. I wasn't scared about the water but worried about coming too close to the grating at the bottom of the pool; I feared that if I got too close, I would get sucked in.*

Sometimes students admit their reaction caused friction with their parents:

One of two frightful experiences I had with television when I was younger was viewing A Nightmare on Elm Street. *I was probably only in second grade when I viewed it. The basic premise was that there was a killer who attacked you in your dreams, but could actually kill you by doing this. He wore a glove with knives attached, and he typically kept this in the basement, usually near the furnace.*

After this incident, I would not go down into our basement, which isn't very creepy, it's decorated. This lasted several months. Once I was willing to go downstairs in the furnished part, I was still petrified to go into the back storage pantry, where our furnace was also located. This made my mom angry because for many years I was too afraid to go in the back room to get food for her. I remember clearly the first time I was actually brave enough to venture there with a flashlight to see near the furnace, and it wasn't until I was in junior high school. To this day, I am still a bit wary of basements, not because they are creepy but because I imagine the possibility that someone really is lurking there like in the movie.

Sometimes students express intense frustration at their reactions:

I was so affected by this movie [Creepshow 2], that I was afraid of going into any of the lakes around my house in fear that an unsuspecting group of lily pads might turn out to be a killer blob. To tell you the truth, since the time I saw that movie, I have honestly never swum in a lake again nor have I gotten up the guts to watch that segment again. If that is not a fright reaction, fifteen years of avoiding lakes because of a stupid movie, then I don't know what is.

What's a Parent to Do?

Why didn't the parents prevent this from happening? you might ask. Good question. A lot of the parents probably did not know it was happening until it was too late. A repeated theme in many students' reports is that they watched without their parents' knowledge and that they were hesitant to admit they'd been frightened. Our research shows that although many parents are left in the dark, so to speak, many mothers and fathers know about their children's fears all too well, like those whose stories have been reported in this chapter.

To explore more systematically what parents know, or think they know, about children's fright reactions, my colleagues and I recently conducted a phone survey in Madison, Wisconsin, calling a random sample of close to three hundred parents who had children in kindergarten through sixth grade. Quite a sizable number (43 percent) of these parents reported that their child had been frightened by something on television and that the fear had lasted beyond the time of viewing. Given the tendency of many children to keep their fear to themselves, these parents' reports may be merely the tip of the iceberg. The stories they told revealed an array of fright reactions similar to those I see in students' papers: One child vomited and could not sleep after watching *Are You Afraid of the Dark?*; another stopped helping his mother cook, something he had previously enjoyed, after seeing a *Rescue 911* episode in which a child was burned while cooking; another refused to participate in any outdoor activity after seeing *My Girl*, a movie in which the popular child actor Macaulay Culkin plays a character who dies after being attacked by a swarm of bees; two children were so scared by TV shows that they were uncomfortable going anywhere alone; and one child began hiding inside the house after viewing *The X-Files*, fearful that someone was watching her. Night terrors, sleep disturbances, fear of the dark, fear of going to bed alone, and clinging to parents in tears were fairly common responses.

The movies parents named as frightening on this survey ranged from Disney movies such as *Dumbo* and *Sleeping Beauty* to *Ghostbusters, Kindergarten Cop,* and *Silence of the Lambs.* Many parents were surprised by their children's intense reactions and felt powerless when it came to stemming the source. One mother, for example, said it bothered her that there were no warnings before advertisements for frightening or violent movies, which can pop up on TV at almost any time.

What the phone survey suggests, then, is that these adverse effects exist not just in the memories of college students. They are important enough and obvious enough to have been noticed by many parents. Although many children undoubtedly keep their distress to themselves, quite a few involve their parents in their problem either by choice or because they can't help it.

Why There's No Easy Solution

After reading all these examples of children who have been traumatized by such a wide variety of television and film offerings, you might be wondering if there is any escape from these horrors, short of donating your TV to charity. The distressing fact is, however, that even if yours is one of the few families who don't have a TV or who guard their children's access to it with vigilance, what your child sees is not always in your control.

For one thing, many children like to watch scary programs, and some will try to overcome parental restrictions. Students' reports are full of inventive ways they have found to see forbidden shows without their parents' knowledge.

For another, young children are often exposed to what their older brothers and sisters or baby-sitters are watching. And even the most cautious and aware parents can't always prevent their children from seeing scary shows at the homes of friends or at school or day care. Different families, teachers, and caregivers often have different attitudes about television. Many parents are hesitant to convey their restrictions to the parents of their children's friends for fear of looking old-fashioned or being perceived as controlling.

Even assuming, though, that what your child sees is largely within your control, there are still complicating issues that need to be faced. "Just don't let your children watch horror movies or scary TV shows," you might say. But it's not that simple. It is often very hard for parents to predict what will disturb their children. "I had no idea it would scare him!" is a frequent refrain. Can a parent be fairly blamed for expecting a movie called *Willy Wonka and the Chocolate Factory*—or, for that matter, *Sleeping Beauty* or *Dumbo*—to be benign? The way children see things and make sense of them is very different from the way we adults see the world and reason about it—an idea I will explain in detail over the course of this book.

"But my child knows what's real and what's make-believe," you might say. Again, things are not as straightforward as they appear. As this book will explain, younger children have a difficult time differentiating fantasy from reality. And even when they begin to know what's real and what's make-believe, there are many reasons why make-believe is scary, too.

And then there's the news, which is *not* make-believe. News stories about such horrors as the Persian Gulf War, the Oklahoma City bombing, the abduction and murder of children, and even tornadoes, floods, and earthquakes have been deeply upsetting to many children. A vigilant parent might avoid watching the news with children around, but what about that dreaded bulletin about the terrorist bombing of a jetliner that can crop up at any moment? Real stories such as these, that raise genuine threats to all of us, are especially challenging for parents to help their children handle.

Finally, entertainment fare in general has become more graphic and horrifying. The myriad cable channels and booming video-rental business ensure that there is virtually no escape from at least occasional exposure to frightening TV shows and movies. Even advertisements for scary movies have left some children traumatized.

For all these reasons, you need advice not only on how to prevent your child's fright reactions but also on the best ways to help your child cope with something scary while watching it and the best strategies to deal with your child's fright once it occurs.

How This Book Can Help

I want to say at the outset that my goal in writing this book is not to launch a crusade against all potentially scary TV and movie material. I am not out to ban *Snow White,* for example, simply because some young children have night-mares about the wicked queen. Rather, by examining this long-neglected topic, I wish to accomplish four things:

Sound an alert for parents. You may not know how much frightening material your child is viewing or whether it's causing more harm than you realize. Unless you know how pervasive media-induced fright reactions are and how intense and long-lasting they can be, you probably won't know how important it is to be careful about what your child views. And you may not know the right questions to pose when he wakes up in the middle of a nightmare or suddenly refuses to engage in an activity you thought he enjoyed.

Help you predict the kind of material that is likely to scare your child. I will use concepts from developmental psychology to explain which aspects of TV shows and movies frighten children at different ages, and why. Chil-dren and adults have different ways of interpreting what they see, and parents who wish to make sensible judgments about what their child can handle must learn to consider material from a child's point of view. Providing you with this knowledge will help you decide for yourself whether a particular movie or TV show may be too scary for your child—and reduce your need to rely on reviewers, marketing campaigns, your child's friends, or other parents. I hope it will also give you confidence in your own judgments and help you communicate the basis for your choices in a way that seems reasonable to the other people who take care of your children.

Guide you in calming your child's fears. Based on the many studies and interviews I have conducted and on principles of child development, I will explain different techniques for calming fears and show how some strategies that work for older kids are ineffective for younger ones and vice versa. In addition, by explaining the reasons why certain techniques are appropriate for certain ages, I hope to enable you to tailor your own coping strategies to the specific needs of your child.

Advise you on how best to shield your child from traumatic content. Your child may *want* to watch scary programs even if they produce negative side-effects. I'll explain some of the psychological reasons for this, discuss ways to communicate tactfully about viewing restrictions, and describe some additional resources available to parents, such as program ratings and TV-blocking technologies.

One way I believe that this book will distinguish itself from other literature you have read on children and television is that I will not just be giving advice; I will be explaining the psychology behind the advice so that you can apply these principles to new programs and in new situations. My conclusions are based not only on the findings of others but on fifteen years of my own research, including observations of children as they watch television, surveys of parents, and the vivid recollections of hundreds of young adults as they look back on their earlier fright experiences.

It is my greatest hope that parents, grandparents, teachers, and other caregivers will turn to this book for aid and comfort—and pass that on to the children in their lives.

CHAPTER TWO

Through a Child's Eyes

....

"I Had No Idea It Would Be So Scary"

Why is it so hard to know when your child will be frightened by TV? There are two big issues here. One is that when our children are not under our direct supervision, they see programs we might restrict them from viewing if we knew they were watching them. The other is that, even when we are aware of what our children are watching, it is difficult for most parents to predict what will frighten them.

Why We Don't Know What They're Watching

When I was about six or seven years old my parents went out for the evening and left me with a baby-sitter. The CBS network was carrying a movie that night which dealt with a literal swarm of tarantulas taking over a small town and biting all of the inhabitants until they

succumbed to the poison of the tarantulas' venom. My
parents had instructed the baby-sitter to not let me watch
this film, but the baby-sitter was watching it and I just
went into the room and sat down. She did nothing to
stop me. . . . While the scenes were a little frightening
then, the feelings have remained, and every time I see a
spider I think of this movie. . . . [O]verall, it is hard to
believe that exposure to this one film fifteen years ago
could have this lasting effect.

An undeniable fact of family life is that most parents
do not have total control over their children's exposure to
television and films. With busy, working parents, multiple
TV sets in the home, and media available at schools, day
care, and at the houses of friends, very few parents have
the security of knowing exactly when their children are
watching TV or what they're viewing. And, even if your
child is not especially interested in watching scary material, there are many forces that make it more likely that
your child will come upon something distressing.

Our retrospective study of college students showed
that more than half of those who reported a long-term
fright reaction had not particularly wanted to see the program that had caused them to be so upset. They saw it for
other reasons. Often, we see what I have come to call the
baby-sitter effect, which was exemplified at the beginning
of this chapter.

Another frequent scenario is that older brothers and

sisters are interested in a scary movie, and the younger siblings just happen to be there. One young man reported
on his younger sister's fright response and said he still felt
responsible for what had happened to her many years
earlier:

> When Poltergeist *came out on cable in the early*
> *1980s, my brother, my younger sister, and I sat down in*
> *front of the television to watch this unexpected horror*
> *film. My brother and I were fine, but my younger sister*
> *was affected by this movie in an extreme way. My sister*
> *was around ten years old when she experienced this film*
> *and it wasn't till she was thirteen that she was able to*
> *fall asleep in her bed rather than in our mother and*
> *father's. . . . Today, I really feel terrible for my sister that*
> *she had to go through this. Is it possible that she would*
> *be a different person today if she hadn't watched the*
> *scariest movie of all time, according to her?*

Often children see frightening movies at a friend's
house. Sometimes the absence of parental restrictions is
coupled with peer pressure to be brave and macho:

> When I was seven years old, I watched (although it
> felt like I witnessed) Friday the Thirteenth, Part 2.
> My family didn't have cable television or any movie
> channels but my friend Mark's family did. One day, just
> he and I watched Jason Voorhees chop up and mutilate

a camp full of oversexed teenagers. I hadn't seen an R-rated movie before this gruesome experience. It blew me away. I stayed for the entirety of the film because I didn't want Mark to think I was a "wussy," and I was also morbidly fascinated by something I'd never been exposed to. After viewing the film, I had nightmares for weeks. I would even lie awake at night (with all the lights on) wondering how long it would take Jason and his twenty-inch blade to find me!

Even a movie promo can induce lasting fears:

When I was about eleven years old there was a movie on TV called The Burning Bed. *It was, I believe, the story of an abused wife who gets fed up and douses her husband with gasoline while he's sleeping. She starts the bed on fire and he burns to death (I assume). I never watched the movie but I saw the ad for it on TV and it scared me to death. . . . I never really worried that someone would start my bed on fire, but I was suddenly certain that we were going to have a house fire which would eventually reach my bedroom and my bed. I would lie awake as long as I could, trying to stay alert, trying to smell the smoke that I knew was going to come creeping under my door.*

Although many fright stories reveal that children's exposure to scary movies was due to chance or to the viewing

choices of people around them, quite a few others tell
about children who really wanted to see the movie that ultimately scared them. Many students report viewing in secret, against their parents' wishes:

> *When I was about ten years old my mother and
> father were planning to watch* An American Werewolf
> in London *on television. . . . I wanted to stay up and
> watch it with them. My mother explained to me that she
> did not feel that it would be a good idea. Needless to say,
> I was upset and determined to watch the man turn into
> a werewolf. They put me to bed and the movie started. I
> waited fifteen minutes and then sneaked into our living
> room. My parents could not see me because the couch was
> positioned with their backs to me.*

The young girl who confessed this intrigue watched the
movie for only about a half hour and returned to her bed
without getting caught. But her fright response prevented
her from pulling off her caper successfully:

> *That night I had an awful dream. I dreamt that a
> pack of werewolves was surrounding my bed. They were
> all drooling blood and growling. They did not jump on
> my bed to eat me, so I felt safe. This allowed me to dream
> that I was going back to sleep again. But then I realized
> that I had to go to the bathroom. Here was the problem:*

If I relieved my bodily function properly, I would be eaten and slashed by many werewolves. Therefore, I could not get off my bed. This dream seemed so real to me that I actually ended up peeing in my bed. I explained to my mother what happened. I got grounded, but we remember this episode as if it happened yesterday.

Why We Can't Tell What They're "Seeing"

Perhaps many adults would expect shows like *Friday the Thirteenth* and *Poltergeist* to be scary, at least if they saw them first. Presumably if parents had been aware that their children were viewing these shows, they might not have been surprised by their reactions. But many other offerings that produce fright seem utterly harmless. *Little House on the Prairie* is a prime example of a title that sounds just too family-friendly to invite parental concern. (I've noticed that students are especially embarrassed to mention that program in class discussions of their fright, particularly because of its name and reputation.) Parents who are trying to be vigilant are often misled by titles, advertising and promotional gimmicks, the presence of a particular actor, the source or studio producing a movie, or a movie's Motion Picture Association of America (MPAA) rating. One concerned parent describes being mistakenly reassured:

My children had been wanting to see the movie Jumanji *since it starred Robin Williams and they had*

enjoyed watching other Robin Williams movies like Mrs.
Doubtfire. *It seemed, from the previews I'd seen, to be
an entertaining movie for children. It was rated PG. I
hadn't heard anything negative about it, so we rented it.
My thirteen-year-old thought it was funny and enjoyed it
immensely. My eight-year-old was a bit fearful of it but
still entertained by it. My six-year-old, who's normally
very daring and adventurous, was terrified of the ele-
phants and rhinoceroses and other huge animals chasing people through houses and refused to leave my side
the rest of the day, despite my assurances that it was just
a movie and couldn't really happen.*

This mother was facing a problem that is confronted
by most families with more than one child: the difficulty
of selecting a movie that will entertain the older children
without traumatizing the younger ones. I will return to
this problem in a later chapter because there's no easy solution to it. For a large portion of what is available in the
media, what is right for one age group is definitely wrong
for another.

In addition, this mother was relying on the MPAA rating of PG: "Parental Guidance Suggested," and she assumed that the movie would be relatively mild in its
impact. In a later chapter, I will discuss this rating system
in more detail and explain why it is so hard to rely on
movie ratings in making viewing choices for children.

Even G-rated movies, those that are supposed to be for "General Audiences," including children, often aren't that safe for young children. Most parents mistakenly assume that a G rating means there's nothing to worry about. Animated, G-rated fairy tale and adventure features provide a good example of this misunderstanding. These movies are a staple of preschooler entertainment, yet when viewed by young children, they often produce fears that last well beyond the time of viewing. I have received reports of children's persistent fears related to many of these features, from *Bambi, Dumbo,* and *Pinocchio* to *Beauty and the Beast* and *The Hunchback of Notre Dame.* Parents who report their children's reactions to these movies are often surprised by the intensity of their child's response.

Why not attack fairy tales, then, you might ask? You may have heard the argument that children's folk stories, and fairy tales, in particular, have always had scary and gruesome elements. Some well-known psychoanalysts have proposed that these stories allow children to work through "traumas that are seething in the unconscious." First, let me say that I have never seen any evidence that fairy tales have this positive effect. But even if such "unconscious" effects might occur from hearing or reading fairy tales, reading a story or being read to is very different from watching television and movies, particularly for young children.

One way in which written fairy tales differ from television and movies is in the way they are usually received by the child. Children who are old enough to read the words can pace themselves according to how much they can handle, and the story will become only as frightening as their imagination lets it be. But, in any event, most children are first exposed to fairy tales by listening to an adult read the words to them. In viewing situations, in contrast, the adult mediator is gone, and often no adult is present at all.

I remember the first time I read the book version of Disney's *Snow White and the Seven Dwarfs* to my then four-year-old son. Although I myself had seen the movie as a child, I couldn't help being unnerved as I read aloud that the wicked queen ordered the huntsman to cut out Snow White's heart because she was jealous of the girl's beauty. I found myself doing a bit of selective editing then and there, doling out the story in smaller, gentler doses, because I was sensitive to the impact it would have. I also noticed how frightening my son found some of the visual images in the book, which were stills taken from the animated Disney feature. I was very glad he was first exposed to this story with me as a "translator" and reassuring presence, rather than having the movie or video version thrust upon him full force.

Had he first seen the movie or video, he would have seen the entire story (or all that he could take!) without editing for his needs, and the visual images would not only have been larger, they would have been in motion. Illustrations in a book are generally less frightening than motion pictures because our brains are wired to react more intensely to moving images (especially threatening images that seem to be coming toward us). I particularly remember my own fear as a child watching *Snow White* when the heroine was lost in the forest. What at first looked like normal trees suddenly sprouted bright yellow eyes and took on the appearance of monsters that grabbed at her as she tried unsuccessfully to escape. Animated adventure features are especially full of grotesque, evil characters who move rapidly and threateningly toward their intended victims and seemingly toward the viewing audience as well.

One young man's memory illustrates the intensity of a child's reaction to a classic Disney film:

> *When I was seven my sister took me to a showing of* Alice in Wonderland. *Throughout the movie I felt uncomfortable with the world that Alice was blundering through. One thing that really frightened me was the grinning Cheshire Cat character. Its evil smile and hissing speech had a lasting effect on me. For years afterward I was afraid of cats and don't care for them even now. But the most intense fear that I have ever experienced was the portion of the movie where Alice is captured by the Queen and her army of "card-men." When the Queen screamed, "Off with her head!" I snapped. I started to cry*

*and hid beneath my seat, cowering from the images on the
screen. I remember being unable to sleep well for about a
week after the experience. My parents had to go to great
lengths to assure me that no one was going to behead me
while I slept. . . . One thing that I think had an impact
on the intensity of my experience was the fact that my parents were not sitting next to me. Without them I was literally at the mercy of the images on the screen.*

But why is it, you may ask, that young children respond so intensely to these apparently fun, animated, totally unrealistic movies? Don't they know (and don't we
tell them often enough) that what is shown in them is totally unreal and could never happen? Isn't it unreasonable
for children to be frightened by these movies that are intended mainly for their entertainment? What's going on
here?

What's going on here is that young children are viewing these movies through a child's eyes. What we are seeing as adults and what they are seeing as children are, for
all intents and purposes, entirely different movies. It is
difficult for parents, but extremely important, to be able
to see television and movies in the way their child will see
them.

The young man who recalled his reaction to *Alice in
Wonderland* showed some insight into this issue while trying to explain the intensity of his reaction:

A small child tends to believe what is presented to him and take it at face value. I took the Cheshire Cat and the beheading to be real and transferred it to my own life.

The Importance of Understanding Child Development

I became interested in studying children's fright reactions to television partly because of the unpredictability of these effects. I didn't find it especially odd that people were having nightmares from *Jaws* or *Psycho,* but it intrigued me that so many parents were perplexed about their children's reactions to movies and programs that they did not expect would frighten them. I also found it fascinating that children of different ages seemed to be frightened by different *types* of programs and events. It might seem logical to expect that the youngest children would be the most frightened by just about every scary image, and that as children matured, all media offerings would become less frightening. But this is not what I was observing. As children get older, some things become less frightening, but other things that have not been disturbing in the past suddenly begin to terrorize.

My approach was to turn to developmental psychology for insights. What do child psychologists know, I wondered, about how children see and reason about the world at different ages? To begin to answer this question I immersed myself in the writings of Jean Piaget, the Swiss psychologist who is generally credited with being the founder of the field of developmental psychology. Like many great researchers, Piaget stumbled onto the field that he made his life's work somewhat by accident.

Early in his career, Piaget was hired to help produce items for intelligence tests. In other words, he was developing questions that would reflect children's intellectual development. What came to fascinate Piaget more than differentiating between the smarter kids, who got the right answers, and the less smart kids, who did not, was the types of errors that young children made consistently. You might expect, for example, that up to a certain age, children would not know the right answer to a particular problem and that they therefore would be uncertain or choose a variety of wrong responses. Instead, what Piaget observed was that for some tasks, the young children who got them wrong would respond without hesitation. And not only would they be sure they were right, they would all choose the same "wrong" answer. What adults saw as the wrong answer was clearly "right" for them.

A typical task involved showing children two ball-shaped globs of clay that were the same size. After getting them to agree that both balls had the same amount of clay, Piaget would let them watch as he rolled one of the balls out into a long, thin, snake shape. Then he would ask whether they both still had the same amount of clay or whether one had more than the other. Piaget found that four- and five-year-olds usually replied without hesitation that the clay in the form of the snake had more. Nine- and ten-year-olds almost always recognized that the two globs of clay had the same amount. From observing many examples like this, Piaget became fascinated with what these younger children were seeing that their older counterparts were not, and he spent the rest of his eighty-odd years observing and chronicling how children of different ages see the world around them and make sense of it.

What, you may now be asking, does the shape of globs of clay have to do with children's fright reactions to television? Piaget did not focus on the topic of children's fears, but as I read about his research and the generalizations he made about children's thought processes, I couldn't help thinking that the types of viewing and reasoning differences Piaget observed in children would have direct effects on their emotional reactions to the images and events they received through television. What particularly fascinated me about these differences was that many of them weren't intuitively obvious. By the time we become adults, we forget many aspects of the way the world seemed to us as children.

What follows in the next few chapters is an examination of some of the major patterns that Piaget and other developmental psychologists have observed in the way children of different ages see the world and reason about it, and how these can be applied to understanding children's emotional reactions to television. In addition to explaining these concepts and giving examples, I will report

on the research I have done that confirms these principles. I will also explain how you can use this information
in guiding your children's viewing and helping them cope
with any unwanted reactions they may have.

Of Ages, Stages, and Your Uniquely
Individual Child

Before getting started on the specifics of how some basic
principles of child development can help you understand
your child's reactions to television, I want to inject a few
words of caution about the use of age guidelines. One way
in which research on child development is sometimes misunderstood is that people expect age guidelines to be absolute and inflexible. As you well know, not all children
develop at exactly the same rate. Most age guidelines used
in this book should be considered broad trends around
which most children will group, but for which there may
be many exceptions. For example, the age at which a child
begins to be more frightened by real than by fantasy figures
(as discussed in chapter 5) may vary somewhat from child
to child. But it should be helpful to know that preschool
children are generally more frightened by fantasy figures,
and that by the end of elementary school most children
are more frightened by things that could really happen.

Another thing to keep in mind is that although this
book will focus on specific aspects of television programs,
one at a time, all programs contain many elements that
work together to affect the emotions of children. A fan-

tasy program may be extremely vivid or not; it may contain eerie-sounding music or not; and it may deal with an issue that is of concern to your child at the moment of viewing or the whole idea may be entirely new. For example, a girl who we might otherwise expect to be too old or too young to react intensely to a particular type of show might be frightened because it relates to something that is currently going on in her family. In short, although we will be considering various elements of programs separately, they must be thought of as part of a whole when determining whether a particular program scares a particular child.

And, of course, we must never forget that you are the person who knows your child the best, and all the advice here should be considered in the context of what you already know about your child. Your child may be outgoing and adventurous or shy and hesitant to try new things. She may love or hate roller coasters, and she may be a sound sleeper or one whose sleep is easily disturbed. She may live in a dangerous neighborhood or in peaceful surroundings. She may or may not have already been exposed to the death or severe illness of family members. And she may already love or hate to watch scary things on television.

Finally, you may have more than one child, and even children in the same family can differ dramatically. All of the guidelines I will be providing here will need to be filtered through a knowledge of each child's personality and experiences. You may have one child for whom scary programs are a problem, and another who can't seem to get enough of them. This entire book should be helpful to you in dealing with your easily frightened child, but parts will also enhance your understanding of your thrill seekers. In that particular regard, chapters 9, 10, and 11 deal with why children like scary programs and how parents can discourage them from overexposure without accidentally making these programs more tantalizing.

With these considerations in mind, let us move on to some specifics of how young children's manner of thinking and seeing makes them respond with fright to programs and movies that few adults would expect to be traumatic.

CHAPTER THREE

Appearance,
Appearance, Appearance

Beauty's More Than Skin Deep

*Even though the amazing powers of the Bionic Woman
saved the day, the image of the monster stayed with me.
Time and again my dreams contained at least some
slow-motion footage of the creature that would cause me
to wake up with a start.*

A Picture's Worth a Million Words

About the time I was beginning to look at children's
fright reactions from the perspective of child development, my husband and I built an addition onto our
house. Toward the beginning of the construction process,
an old friend dropped by with his three-year-old son, Sam.
As we sat on our deck reminiscing about old times, Sam's
attention became fully fixated upon the large crater in the

ground right next to where we were sitting. The sight was, objectively speaking, horrible. Right after the construction crews had dug the hole, we had had torrential rains, and the area was in complete disarray. With the demolition work that had been carried out in preparation for the construction, the yard looked more like the site of a bombing than the place where a handsome new room would soon be built. Sam repeatedly interrupted us, asking the same question over and over. "What's that hole?" he would say, and we would repeatedly answer, saying something like "That's where they're going to build our new living room." During each explanation, Sam would turn toward us and away from the hole, and then nod his head as if he understood. But the next time he turned his head and saw the hole, the explanation would evaporate from his mind, and he would anxiously ask the same question again. After repeated attempts on our part to explain what the hole was for, and after a good deal of irritation on the part of Sam's father, we simply gave up.

Although we failed to reassure Sam, my familiarity with Piaget made me realize that he was exhibiting an important characteristic of the way preschool children react to the world around them: The visual image Sam was dealing with was simply too powerful to be explained away in words.

Research shows that very young children respond to things mainly in terms of how they appear. When Piaget tried to analyze young children's reactions to different-shaped globs of clay, he reasoned that one of their problems was that the longer, thinner glob *looked* bigger. A follower of Piaget noted that young children focus on and react to whatever "clamors loudest for their attention," often ignoring other things that are available to see and hear. In the clay test, the length of the glob seems to grab children's attention more easily than its circumference.

In general, what clamors loudest for the young child's attention is whatever is the most immediately and easily perceived—whatever is the most vividly visual or makes the most intense noise and whatever needs no learning or interpretation to appreciate. Often what grabs the child's attention the most is what something looks like, but sometimes sounds that are striking or peculiar do the same thing. I'll focus first on the effect of visual appearance because we know the most about this.

If you ask preschool children to group a set of pictures according to which things go together, they will usually match items that look alike. They might pair things that are the same color or the same size or the same shape and show little concern for things that belong together for other reasons. Suppose we give preschoolers four pictures: a blue hammer, a red saw, a blue fork, and a red plate. These children are likely to match the two red things and the two blue things. But as they come closer to the age of seven or so, they are more and more likely to say that the hammer goes with the saw and the fork goes with the plate because older children give color less importance and begin to think about things belonging together that are used together or have a similar function. Color is a much more obvious visual characteristic of these items; their function is something that is learned over time.

The implications of these findings for the types of things that should frighten children on television seemed clear to me. If young children react most strongly to the appearance of things when they are asked to sort them, shouldn't looks count the most heavily in what frightens them? If this is the case, things that *look* scary should be the most frightening to preschool children. The first thing my colleagues and I did to explore this idea was to ask parents which programs and movies had frightened their children the most. We gave a written questionnaire to parents of children from eleven preschools and eight elementary schools, asking them to list the television shows or movies that had caused the most fear and distress in their child. The results suggested that I might be right. What frightened preschoolers the most according to parents? *The Incredible Hulk,* an adventure program starring a monstrous-looking superhero, and *The Wizard of Oz.* Both of these shows feature grotesque, green-faced, scary-looking characters.

We can see the importance of appearance in the retrospective reports of many college students who remember their fear of the Hulk:

> *I can still vividly recall every detail—the green skin,*
> *the bulging biceps, and the gnarly black mop of hair.*

Similarly, when college students talk about their nightmares from *The Wizard of Oz,* many of them emphasize the frightening appearance of the Wicked Witch of the West. Here are some typical examples:

> *For me, the thing that topped all of these was the*
> *Wicked Witch of the West from the movie classic* The
> Wizard of Oz. *Her scary, screeching voice, her green*
> *skin, her broomstick, and her big black hat all haunted*
> *me for years after first seeing the movie at age six.*

> *The witches and the monkeys caused me to either*
> *run out of the room or at least close my eyes. . . . The im-*
> *ages are so vivid with the witch's green face and ugly fea-*
> *tures along with that horrifying voice and laugh.*

Many other memories of fright experienced by young children also focus on visual aspects of the terror-producing movie or TV show. Here's a typical example:

> *When I was five or six years old, I viewed the movie*
> Tarantulas. *It was a black-and-white B-rated* [sic] *film*
> *that would strike many people as either funny or silly if*
> *viewed at an older age. The contents of the movie escape*
> *my mind except that I am still left with the lingering*

image of an ungodly-sized tarantula walking over a city
as mass crowds run from the forthcoming destruction. . . .
Nothing has scared me quite like that since, and I some-
times wonder if my keen dislike of spiders and spidery
things stems from my initial step past the boundaries of
reality, dealing with that tarantula.

The next example shows a college student's memory of watching *Star Trek* when he was four years old. Note the striking detail of the writer's memory and his keen emphasis on the visual images:

Throughout the entire episode, people dropped like
flies, yet watching the corpses pile up is not what truly ter-
rified me. What sent shivers up my spine was seeing what
this "salt vampire" really looked like. Ugly would have
been an understatement. This creature had deeply inset
black eyes, a large gaping mouth which sported several
sharp fangs, and was covered from head to toe with long,
unkempt, dirty gray hair. Another notable feature was the
creature's suction cup–like "salt-suckers" on its palms
and fingers, which it used to extract the victim's salt di-
rectly from their face (yeech!). I distinctly remember that
those "suckers" unnerved me more than anything else.
This was easily the scariest thing that this particular
four-year-old had ever seen. The image of this grotesquely
hideous creature kept me awake the entire night. I had

*this fear that a salt vampire was going to grab me from
underneath my bed, suck out my face, and end my life.*

When Appearance Competes with
Other Factors

Although the anecdotes were fascinating and the survey
research was encouraging, I knew I needed to study the effect of appearance more systematically. Older children
and adults are also sometimes upset by gory, grotesque
images. What I really wanted to know was whether young
children are *more* sensitive to grotesque visual images than
older children. Although we had many more examples of
intense reactions to scary-looking characters in younger
than in older children, my colleagues and I answered the
question about how sensitive to appearance different age
groups are by doing a controlled experiment.

As I explained earlier, developmental research on
matching tasks shows that in addition to being more likely
to respond to how things look, preschool children are less
likely than older children to respond to other aspects of a
situation. As children move into the middle and later
elementary-school years, they give other types of information more weight—information that is not as closely tied
to appearance. What we wanted to do in our research,
then, was to test the idea that younger children are more
sensitive to the appearance of characters than older children, and that older children are more sensitive than

younger children to other aspects of a program, such as what the character says or does or the character's good or evil intentions.

We produced a video in four versions so that we could systematically vary both the appearance and the behavior of a character while leaving the story identical in every other respect. In our video, the main character, an old woman, was created with two very different appearances: She appeared either ugly and witchlike or attractive and grandmotherly. In the story, the old woman was seen to behave either kindly or cruelly.

The story involves two curious children who enter an old woman's house, uninvited, to retrieve their wandering dog. When they suddenly hear her voice, they hide under her dining-room table and watch as she discovers a stray cat in her front hall. In the "kind" scenario, the old woman welcomes the cat, cuddling it in her arms, and cheerfully feeds it a bowl of cream. In the "cruel" scenario, she yells at the cat, throws it down the basement stairs, and threatens to starve it. The video does not have a true ending. The tape stops just as the old woman is about to find the children.

There were four versions of the story: one in which the main character was ugly and kind; one in which she was ugly and cruel; one in which she was attractive and kind; and one in which she was attractive and cruel. In the experiment, we showed our videos to children in three age groups. The youngest children were between three and five; children in the middle group were six or seven; and those in the oldest group were nine or ten. Each child saw only one of the four versions.

What we found in this experiment was just what we expected. When we asked the children to rate how nice or mean the old lady was, the youngest group was most affected by how the old woman looked and least affected by how she had behaved. On the whole, the youngest children tended to think the woman was nice when she was attractive and mean when she was ugly. As the age of the children increased, the woman's looks made less and less of a difference. At the same time, the woman's behavior became more important as the children got older. In addition, when they were asked to predict what the woman would do to the children when she found them, the youngest group was strongly affected by the way she looked. Her pleasant looks made them more likely to say she would serve the children cookies, and her ugly looks made more of them think she would lock them up in a closet! Older children's expectations were not affected by what she looked like. Only her prior behavior influenced their predictions.

It is important to note that this study did not show that appearances never affect the reactions of older children. In fact, we did a second study where we showed children pictures of the old woman and asked them how they expected her to behave in a TV program. Without information about her behavior, children in all three age groups expected the ugly woman to be mean and the attractive woman to be nice. All children, and even adults, engage in stereotyping to some extent. What the first experiment showed is that when a situation involves both vivid appearances *and* other information that is less obviously visual, younger children are more influenced by appearance and less influenced by the other information than older children are.

As a generalization, then, we can say that preschool children are more likely to be frightened by something that looks scary but is actually harmless than by something that looks attractive but is actually harmful. As children get older, they come to understand that looks and behavior may be inconsistent, and they are frightened by things that cause harm but do not necessarily have a vivid visual presence. *The Amityville Horror* is a good example of a movie with a dangerous but largely invisible evil force. In the survey we conducted in the early eighties, this movie was reported to have scared many more older children than younger ones.

The Day After is another good example of a movie that frightened older children more than younger ones because the threat it depicted was more abstract than vividly visual. This made-for-TV movie depicted a Kansas community in the aftermath of a nuclear attack. Prior to its airing, the program was described as "bringing the unwatchable to TV" and "the starkest nightmare ever broadcast."

Although some national education groups and many elementary schools urged that younger children be shielded from viewing the movie, we felt that this advice was misplaced. The movie's major theme involves the abstract threat of nuclear annihilation, with the real horror of the movie coming from the contemplation of the end of civilization as we know it. These are terrifying concepts, yet they are beyond the mental capacity of the young child and cannot be conveyed in pictures.

Contrary to general expectations, we thought the movie would be more terrifying the more the viewer had the mental capacity to grasp these abstract themes. When we conducted a random phone survey of parents the night after the movie aired, we found that children under twelve were much less disturbed by the film than were teenagers. (In fact, the parents reported being more disturbed than their children!) The very youngest children who saw the movie (three- to seven-year-olds) were not at all upset. Indeed, when parents of the youngest group of children were asked whether any TV shows or movies had scared their child more than *The Day After,* they named such apparently benign offerings as the animated movie *Charlotte's Web* and the children's show *Captain Kangaroo.* Parents of teenagers, in contrast, said that *The Day After* had been the most frightening thing their child had seen all year.

These results are not surprising when you consider the cognitive abilities of young children. Public opinion about the movie's effects was based on an adult view of the movie rather than an understanding that young children would be relatively unmoved by the film's abstract, while admittedly devastating, implications.

The Wicked Beauty and the Kindhearted Beast

The fact that preschool children react mainly on the basis of appearance is especially important when they confront situations in which physical appearance contrasts with other aspects of a character or situation. In the typical story where you have an ugly villain and a handsome hero or beautiful heroine, preschool children generally have no problem understanding the intended characterization. But they often react in unexpected ways when the hero is ugly or an evil character is beautiful.

On a personal note, this explains my puzzlement the first time I saw *Gone with the Wind* at about the age of five. I was so impressed with Scarlett O'Hara's beauty that I remember not being able to understand why everybody was criticizing her for being selfish and coldhearted. She was so beautiful, and to me she could do no wrong. It wasn't until I was much older that I could put looks aside and make any sense of the story line.

The monstrous but admirable Incredible Hulk is another good example of a hero bound to be misunderstood by young children. I have even received several retrospective reports from students who were frightened by The Count on *Sesame Street*. Although this muppet is there to teach numbers and not to frighten kids, some children are alarmed by his vampire-like appearance. And of course, there's E.T., that lovable extraterrestrial from the movie of the same name. Many parents have reported how frightened their preschoolers were of the central character of this heartwarming movie. It didn't matter to these children how kind and sweet and helpful E.T. was, nor how many times parents tried to explain the creature's lovable nature; children were still extremely upset.

In trying to predict whether a television show or movie will frighten children up to about six or seven, then, it is most important to first look at the visual images that will confront them. If these images are gory or grotesque, my advice is to wait.

The following description recounts a sad example of the impact of parents not anticipating the power of grotesque visual images:

> *When I was five years old, my parents took me to a drive-in theater to see a movie. They chose an adult-oriented film,* The Elephant Man, *because they thought that I would fall asleep in the car. They regret making that assumption to this day. Surprisingly, I stayed awake through the whole film, absorbing enough of it to be traumatized for the next couple of years. The movie is a true story based on the life of John Merrick, a nineteenth-century Englishman who was afflicted with a disease*

that left him horribly deformed. He became part of a freak show and always wore a paper bag over his head so that people couldn't see his horribly disfigured face. When I saw the Elephant Man in the movie, I thought he was the ugliest, meanest monster I had ever seen. In an attempt to ease my fears, my father would always explain that the Elephant Man wasn't a monster; he was really a nice man that everybody just misunderstood. The Elephant Man would never hurt a little girl, he said, and he couldn't help it that he had a disfiguring disease.

I don't think I or my parents slept very much during the next two years. I had terrible nightmares that the Elephant Man with a paper bag over his head was chasing after me. I would wake up screaming and crying, then I would be too afraid to close my eyes again. I was sure that he was hiding in my closet, under my bed, or behind the shower curtain in the bathroom.

This example is telling not only because of the intensity of the fear that the movie produced, but because it shows how the visual image overpowered the message of the film in this child's mind. Adults, too, might be woefully upset after viewing this movie. As adults, though, we would probably empathize with Merrick as a victim, and perhaps we would feel shame that our society so mistreats individuals whose only crime is to be unsightly. That message was lost on this young child. To her, the Elephant Man was the villain, and he appeared in her dreams as her attacker. This response is not unusual. As we will see in the next chapter, many nightmares about the Incredible Hulk involve fears of being attacked by this benevolent but grotesque creature.

Are Some Images Naturally Scary?

But why are young children so quick to consider certain images scary? Just what makes something attractive or repulsive to a child or, for that matter, to most of us? Many people have noted that beauty is often defined by the norms of a particular culture and that standards of beauty are learned, to a certain extent. There is great variation in what people find beautiful in another person, and no doubt there are great differences in what people call ugly.

But what is it that causes certain visual images to be repulsive and scary instantaneously, even to infants and very young children? Young children do not have to be taught to fear ugly witches and creepy-looking monsters; they do this automatically. And many of us have what seems to be an inbred fear of snakes. Are we born with the predisposition to recoil in terror at certain visual images?

Well, it seems that we are, and there's a good reason for this tendency. If we look at the theory of evolution, it suggests that species that are alive today are here because they had certain characteristics that helped many of them survive long enough to produce offspring. One such tendency might be an innate capacity to fear things that are likely to be harmful and to respond quickly to the sight of danger. An evolutionary view would suggest that the animals we most readily fear, even today, look similar to those that were the most threatening to the survival of our species' ancestors. Research shows that without learning, humans easily become frightened by some things that may or may not be dangerous. Certain types of animals, for example, especially snakes and spiders, more readily evoke fear than other types. Somehow a snake seems easier to fear than a bear, although the bear may well be more dangerous to us. Perhaps because of our evolutionary past, most children find certain animals repulsive and others cute, although they may adjust their reactions as they mature and get to know the animals better.

Other visual images also seem to upset and frighten us automatically. We seem predisposed to be repulsed by the graphic display of injuries. This tendency makes evolutionary sense, too, since the presence of a mutilated corpse or a severely bloodied and injured animal probably meant to our ancestors that a predator was close at hand and that they were in danger as well.

A third type of visual image that automatically repels and scares us is physical deformity. Part of our response may be due to the association of deformities with injuries and disease, and part may be due to the justifiable fear of unknown species. We automatically recoil (even if we learn to control this response as adults) at disfigured faces and deformed limbs. We also respond with distress to distortions of what we come to view as natural. We feel somehow that it is natural to be born with one head, one nose, and one mouth, but two eyes and two ears. We also expect that the head should be attached to the body between the two shoulders. A perfectly normal head attached to the stomach would indeed be disturbing. Deviations from what seems natural are scary. This is where monsters come in.

A monster is simply a distortion of the natural form of a familiar being. Monsters resemble a normal being in many ways but differ in other crucial ways: variations in size (giants and dwarfs), shape (characters with misshapen heads or hunchbacks, for example), skin color or texture (like green faces or hairy bodies), or the number of certain features (one-eyed, three-armed aliens). These things automatically scare us.

And what makes a nondeformed character look scary? Perhaps characteristics that seem likely to be used violently, such as enormous muscles, sharp teeth, and clawlike fingernails. And what makes normal facial features scary? Perhaps the facial features that scare us the most remind us of facial expressions that frighten us, such as those exhibiting anger or fear.

In sum, certain types of animals, the graphic display of injuries, distortions of natural forms, and violent-looking characters all seem designed to immediately upset and frighten us. The makers of horror movies understand this very well and they populate their films with scary images for maximum impact. Young children don't need to be taught to fear them.

What Makes Young Children So Susceptible?

Piaget argued that part of the reason young children react to things differently is biological: The brain actually needs to grow and develop before children can interpret certain things in more mature ways. Although he could not be specific about how the brain functioned or developed, recent findings in neuroscience may now be providing an explanation. Researchers have identified a small part of the brain called the amygdala as the center where innately threatening sights and sounds are received. According to recent research, this region of the brain immediately makes the body respond in fear to certain images, particularly those that signal danger. When this occurs, the body exhibits the so-called fight or flight response, and we experience fear unless or until higher-order processes in other parts of the brain tell it the equivalent of "Never mind, you're not really in danger." The cerebral cortex, where this higher-level processing goes on, is not well developed in younger children. Therefore, it will not be as effective in turning off the immediate fright response. Younger children may remain frightened by the visual image or sound because their brainpower is not sufficient to undo the automatic response. As children get older, however, it seems that their

brains develop enough to begin to override their immediate response to scary images. They may still have an initial response of fear, but it goes away more quickly as they
are able to put it into the perspective of what else they
have come to know. The tendency to be overpowered by
visual images, then, is probably a physiologically based response that must be outgrown. Up to the right age, no
amount of reasoning will take it away.

Of Shrieks, Screams, and Squeaking Violins

What about young children's susceptibility to eerie
sounds? Earlier, I referred to the fact that certain types of
intense or peculiar noises, as well as vivid visual images,
have the capacity to grab young children's attention. You
may remember that the descriptions of the Wicked Witch
at the beginning of this chapter referred to the sounds
she made as well as her looks. Her "screeching voice" and
"horrifying . . . laugh" seemed to traumatize these children as much as her pointy features and green skin. Many,
many retrospective accounts of scary movies recall the
sounds of bloodcurdling yells and musical soundtracks
that mimic the noise of an attack or a victim's screams.

The sounds that readily terrorize young children do
not come from words. They come from auditory cues that
even animals respond to. Long before children learn to
understand and use language, they can differentiate between an angry and a loving tone of voice. Sudden loud,

unexplained noises make all of us jump before we are even consciously aware of them; the roar or growl of a predator and the shrieks and screams of victims evoke fear in animals as they do in us. Again, it seems that we must be responding to the sounds that our ancestors had to be sensitive to in order to survive.

I remember an incident that happened to my family several years ago when we visited the Milwaukee Public Museum. We were relieved to see that our one-and-a-half-year-old son was enjoying many of the static displays of large dinosaurs and stampeding buffaloes. But we weren't prepared for the terror he experienced as we neared the re-creation of a tropical rain forest. Before we even entered that area, Alex cried out in distress and begged us not to go in there. We could tell he was responding to the sounds that were emanating from these rooms. These were the alarm sounds, we figured out later, that monkeys emit when in extreme danger. The sounds did not mean much to us, but they undoubtedly spoke volumes to Alex. No amount of coaxing was able to convince him to enter that space. It seems that in many cases, soundtracks that make our hair stand on end are likely to frighten very young children even if these children don't understand anything about what's going on in the movie.

Taking Your Child's Perspective

The implications of younger children's hypersensitivity to certain sounds and images are dramatic. Young children can be traumatized by brief exposure to a single bizarre visual or auditory image. It is easy to observe this effect on Halloween, when there are many images involving creepy or vicious animals and distorted or gruesomely injured characters. The popular haunted house that children are invited to explore provides a potpourri of all the images and sounds we readily fear. Older children often find this enjoyable. The problem is that for a very young child, these images can echo vividly in their minds, which do not yet have the ability to moderate their effects.

In scary movies and television programs, we see the same thing. Your young child, up to the age of six or seven, is responding most strongly to the most striking images and sounds and is getting much less of the meaning of the story than you or I would. To view a scary program from a young child's perspective, imagine that you're sitting in the front row of a darkened movie theater, that the volume is turned way up, and the dialogue is in a language you don't understand. You are at the mercy of these vivid visual images and sounds and don't have the brainpower to tune them out or reason them away. What is more, as we will see in chapter 5, what you are seeing is real.

Of course, this all suggests being cautious about what we let young children see. But beyond that, it also argues that we should be understanding of and patient with the intensity and duration of our children's responses. They cannot help it if they are overreacting, and they cannot help it if our reassuring words are unable to dim those images. Telling them it's not real or nagging them to snap out of it will not ease their fears. Fortunately, as we will see in later chapters, there are some things that can reduce their fears. But for the reasons I've explained here, nothing we can do for them after the fact comes anywhere near the effectiveness of prevention.

CHAPTER FOUR

The Trouble with Transformations

"All of a Sudden, His Eyes Would Turn a Really Weird Shade of White . . ."

One specific instance in which I can recall being completely and utterly mortified was watching The Incredible Hulk *at the age of about six. I can vividly remember watching the show, in the dark, on the foot of my parents' bed—scared to the point that I had to run out of the room and had a near impossible time going to bed later on. Interestingly, in retrospect,* The Incredible Hulk *was not created to be a frightening program. Whether intended to scare or not, that one instance clearly sticks out in my mind as the most scared I have ever been—even more than at horror movies in which that is the intent.*

If you're familiar with the series *The Incredible Hulk*, but were not in preschool when it aired in the early 1980s, you may be quite surprised at the intensity of this recollected reaction. However, this young child's fright was far from unusual. In fact, *The Incredible Hulk* is one of the most intensely disturbing of the shows I have studied in terms of how profoundly it affected preschool and early-elementary-school children.

Although by now I have received dozens of reports from people who were frightened by this program as children, my interest in *The Incredible Hulk* was stimulated not by reports of children's fear but by Piaget's descriptions of how children between the ages of three and seven respond to the things they see in the world around them. He named this the "preoperational" stage because it occurs before the child can perform some basic mental operations. The stage following the preoperational stage, spanning roughly ages seven to twelve, was termed "concrete operational," recognizing children's ability to perform such operations if a problem is presented in a concrete, perceptible form.

The characteristic of preoperational thought that first caught my attention was what Piaget described as the failure to understand transformations.

What Piaget was talking about was not an emotional response, nor a response to fantasy characters. He was referring to children's performance on test items like the globs-of-clay task I described in chapter 2. Piaget conducted many experiments testing children's ability to "conserve," that is, to see that objects or amounts remain the same even though their physical appearance may change. The classic conservation test began with showing children two identical glasses of water. After children agreed that there was the same amount of water in the two glasses, Piaget would tell the children to watch as he poured the water from one of the glasses into a third glass, of a different shape. Usually the new glass was a lot narrower than the first two glasses, so the water came up to a much higher level. Now Piaget would ask the child whether the new glass contained the same amount as the other glass, sitting right next to it, or whether the new glass had more or less than the other one.

As adults, we know that six ounces of water is six ounces of water, whether it's in a narrow or a wide glass. Yet children under age six or so usually do not see that the amount remains the same, even when the water is poured back and forth before their eyes. Indeed, the overwhelming majority of three- to five-year-olds routinely flunk the conservation test, saying that the narrow glass that's filled to a higher level holds more water. But by the age of nine or ten, almost all children pass this test.

Piaget noted that preschoolers had this same inability to conserve in a variety of physical areas. Not only that, he also found that it was very difficult to train them to get the answer right, even with repeated trials. When attempting to explain what was going on, Piaget proposed that the

young child focuses his attention on the two end states of
the process—in this case, what the water looks like in the
two different glasses. What the child somehow misses is
the process of transformation that links the two (the pour-
ing of the water from one glass to the other).

As I was reading about this research, I could not help
thinking that this failure to understand transformations
might affect children's reactions to the many physical
transformations of characters that occur on television and
in films, particularly in those that are scary. How would
this inability to understand transformations affect children's responses to movies like Disney's *Snow White,* where
the evil queen suddenly turns into a haggard old witch, or
their reactions to werewolf movies, in which normal humans turn into vicious, hairy beasts before the viewer's
eyes? At the time I was thinking about these issues, *The Incredible Hulk* was at the height of its popularity. Because its
plot always showed the normal-looking, attractive main
character suddenly being transformed into a grotesque
monster, I thought to myself, "If Piaget is right about
transformations, young children should have trouble with
the transformation in this program, and that ought to
make it especially scary for them." At the time, I didn't
know quite how scary it was.

I soon discovered how frightening young children
found this program when I looked at the results of the
parent survey we conducted in the spring of 1981. Although we had not suggested any titles—parents simply

wrote in the names of the programs that had scared their child—we found that *The Incredible Hulk* overwhelmed all other programs and movies in the replies of parents of young children. Fully 40 percent of the parents of preschoolers listed *The Incredible Hulk* as a program that had upset their child. In addition, 24 percent of the parents of first graders named it. These were the highest percentages of parents I've ever observed naming any program or movie as scary. And the interesting thing is, *The Incredible Hulk* wasn't supposed to be a scary program. Most parents didn't realize it was scary until their young child let them know about it.

After finding that young children did indeed find this program scary, at least according to their parents, we designed a study to learn more about the reasons for this reaction. We wanted to know, specifically, whether the transformation had something to do with young children's fear.

First, we put together a short video clip based on a typical episode of the program. In the episode we used, the hero, Dr. David Banner (played by the late Bill Bixby), is visiting a hospital when an explosion occurs and a worker is trapped under debris where a fire is quickly spreading. David first tries to lift the fallen objects to free the helpless, frightened worker, but he is not strong enough. Then, a second explosion hurls David against the wall, and this sets off the transformation.

During the transformation, the camera focuses on

David's eyes as the pupils become very small, and then on his arms, shoulders, and muscles, which turn green and grow so fast that they rip out of his shirt. Then the camera shows his feet increasing in size so quickly that they burst through his shoes. Finally, the entire Hulk character is seen throwing off the remains of his tattered shirt. The Hulk (played by body-builder Lou Ferrigno) now has a green face, wild hair, and bushy eyebrows, in addition to a grotesquely muscular physique.

With his superhuman strength, the Hulk easily removes the debris that is trapping the worker, carries him out of danger, and sets him down gently. Then he races through the hospital corridor, inadvertently scaring hospital employees left and right, and exits, growling, by jumping through a plate-glass window.

Once we had put this clip together, we wanted to see whether children whom Piaget would consider preoperational would react differently from children in Piaget's concrete operational stage. So we recruited children in preschool and elementary school to watch our excerpt. The preschool group ranged in age from three to five years; the elementary-school children were nine to eleven years old.

What did we expect to happen? If Piaget was right that preschool children do not understand transformations, we expected that our younger group would not understand that when the Hulk emerges, he is still David, the good guy, and that, in spite of his appearance, he is there to help the victim of the explosion. We predicted, then, that the younger group of children would be most frightened during the portion of the program when the transformation occurred and in the period following it when the monstrous-looking Hulk was on the screen. Also, if, as Piaget led us to believe, the older children were able to understand the transformation, we expected them not to be frightened by this change. On the contrary, these children were expected to be the most frightened during the first part of the excerpt when the hospital worker was injured and when it seemed as though he would be unable to escape before the fire reached him.

We showed this excerpt to the children, one at a time. Immediately after it was over we asked the children to tell us how they had felt during each of the three critical portions of the program. We illustrated each portion for them with stills from the video. What I'll call the "David portion" showed the explosion, the man trapped beneath the debris, and David trying to rescue him. The "transformation portion" showed the Hulk's torso ripping out of his shirt, his feet breaking through his shoes, and the Hulk ripping off his tattered shirt as he emerges from the debris. Finally, the "Hulk portion" showed the Hulk carrying the worker to safety and escaping from the building.

When we looked at children's ratings of how they felt during the different portions of the program, we found exactly what we had expected. Younger children found the program the least scary during the David portion, but

their fear increased somewhat during the transformation, and was at its highest during the portion in which
the grotesque Hulk was shown doing his good deed and
then escaping. The older children showed pretty much
the opposite pattern: They were the most frightened during the David portion, when a character was in danger
and no one was able to help him. Their fear was greatly
reduced during both the transformation portion and the
Hulk portion. These children apparently understood that
David was becoming the superhuman Hulk and that he
was using his powers to rescue the victim. The Hulk's grotesque appearance didn't faze them. Through further
questioning, we also found that although the older children understood what was happening during the transformation, younger children generally were confused
by it.

This study told us that Piaget's observations about
transformations of physical form were helpful in explaining children's fright reactions to a very different type of
transformation on television. The research seemed clear
in isolating the transformation as a central part of young
children's problem with the program. However, because
of how we test children in the lab—showing them only a
short scene and discussing it with them immediately afterward—the study did not give us any hint of how strongly
children were reacting to this program when watching it
at home.

"Tell Me When the Hulk's Gone"

Students who are undergraduates today were preschoolers when the Hulk was at its height of popularity, and I am now receiving numerous accounts of Hulk-reactions from the students in my classes and from other undergraduates participating in my research. The students' retrospective reports show reactions that were surprisingly intense. The following are recent accounts from students who chose *The Incredible Hulk* when asked to talk about a frightening TV experience:

> *I recall that whenever his eyes turned green (the first sign that the Hulk was coming), I would close my eyes, plug my ears, and go sit as close to my mother as I possibly could. I would also say, "Tell me when the Hulk's gone!"*

> *Eventually, in the middle of the show, someone would hurt David Banner and all of a sudden his eyes would turn a really weird shade of white and he would begin to transform into the Hulk. I immediately turned around and hopped on my dad's lap, practically boring a hole in his side, trying to get away from the big green monster. Even though I knew David was safe because of the monster, I was still really freaked out.*

> *Watching the metamorphosis enhanced my fear of the dark. I recall trembling as I walked down the long,*

dark hallway toward my bedroom at the end. I slowly
passed all of the open doorways of dark rooms, inching
closer to my bedroom, thankful as I passed each one that
the Hulk had not been waiting behind a door to thrash
me. Weeks and even months after watching one program,
I was still afraid of walking down the hallway at night.

One thing I find interesting about these retrospective
reports is that all of these students key in on the transformation itself as the main cause of their fright reaction.
Even though this knowledge didn't help them reduce
their fear, they seem to have been quite aware of what it
was about the program that bothered them.

What is perhaps even more surprising about these reports is the intensity with which these children responded
to the transformation. Each of these students reports a
level of fear that we might expect from *Jaws* or *Psycho,* not
from a mild-seeming action-adventure program with few
pretensions of scariness.

Breaking a Fundamental Rule:
The Loss of Trust

Thinking about the intensity of these responses, it seems
clear to me that a simple failure to understand transformations is not sufficient to explain how profoundly this
program frightened children. Not all transformations are
upsetting. No one ever noticed children becoming upset
during Piaget's conservation tests; nor do children ever

seem alarmed when watching a science film showing water turning into ice or a bud becoming a flower. What is it about this transformation of a nice-looking hero into a monster that's so threatening to the young child? One student's description seems to hint at an explanation:

> *After the first few opening sounds, I could sense what was coming as I ran into my parents' bedroom to hide. I became terrified as I watched this perfectly normal and calm human being become transformed into this giant monster in just a matter of seconds. It made me feel like I couldn't trust people or predict what was going to happen next in life.*

When you think about the perspective of young children, it really makes sense that they should be so sensitive to transformations of characters. Their reaction is a lot more than just failing to understand what is going on. As this student suggests, perhaps the transformation represents a breach of trust about a fundamental aspect of the way things are in the world—something they have only recently come to understand and depend on.

Tolstoy once wrote: "From the newborn baby to the child of five is an appalling distance," and he certainly was right. Think of the enormous number of important things a child learns about the world from the time she is born until the preschool years. As you may remember from the birth of your own child, the newborn's behavior is at first a bundle of reflexes and random actions. She doesn't have much sense of the world around her. She doesn't see very well at first, and she reacts only to things that she can perceive directly.

One of the many things that babies learn during the first year is called "object permanence." Show a five-month-old baby a ball and then hide it under a blanket, and to her, it's gone. Over time, the young child learns that things still exist when they can't be seen and that they don't disappear by magic. The concept of "person identity" takes a while to develop, too. Before that concept develops, the baby doesn't realize that her mother is a unique being—that is, she is one and only one person, no matter where she is seen or what she is wearing. This is one reason why parents do not usually observe separation anxiety before their baby is eight or nine months old. Without understanding this basic developmental concept, the mother of a nine-month-old might find it strange that it suddenly seems harder to drop her child off at day care than it was just a month before.

Other concepts related to identity take a long time to develop. For example, in one famous study, children between the ages of three and six were allowed to pet a tame and friendly cat, and then watched its hindquarters while a researcher placed a realistic mask of a vicious dog over the cat's face. Although the animal had never been out of their sight, many of the younger children believed that when the animal turned around, it had become a dog. As you might expect, these children showed more fear in the presence of this "new" animal than their older counterparts, who understood that the new appearance did not change who the animal was or whether it could hurt them. This study illustrates that little by little, children come to understand certain fundamental rules of the physical world. One of these is that people and animals have underlying identities that are not affected by momentary changes in their appearance.

Have you ever seen a toddler mistakenly walk up behind a woman he thinks is his mother and then recoil in horror and burst into tears when she turns around and he sees the stranger's face? If you have ever been that stranger, you may have been struck by the terror in the child's expression, and you may even have asked yourself, "OK, so I'm not his mother, but do I really look that dreadful today?"

Rest assured that you didn't look that bad. The intensity of the child's reaction was not due to any flaws in your physical appearance. To the young child who has not fully grasped the concept of person identity, you were his mother when he grabbed the back of your skirt, but his mother has just been *transformed* into a stranger before his eyes. Talk about scary!

That was the toddler . . . After a while, of course, all children grasp the notion of person identity. By four or five years old, children have learned that this cannot happen. People stay the same—they don't transform into new shapes, colors, or identities before your eyes. *Phew!* That's reassuring.

But then, there's television, where the things we see are a lot like the real world, but once in a while, the rules don't apply. A lot of things that children have spent several years learning by experience no longer work the same way all the time. Take gravity, for example. Children aren't born knowing that if they let something go, it falls to the ground, but over time, with lots of experience, they get the idea. The law that things fall if you let them go is pretty reliable. Of course, it's not always that way on television and in movies. Object permanence doesn't always work on TV, either. On TV, things that are there one second may suddenly disappear the next.

Person identity is another concept that children have come to trust by the time they're four or five. People don't suddenly transform themselves into something or someone else. A mask over someone's face is just a mask. You can pull it off, and it's still Daddy underneath. If you're walking along holding your mother's hand, you won't suddenly look up and find that she's turned into a witch.

So imagine that you're a child who has mastered this reassuring concept and you're watching television. There's a story about a very nice-looking, kind, and thoughtful man. Suddenly this character you've come to like and trust starts to grow very fast, turns green, and becomes a grotesque monster before your eyes—this *is* scary. Maybe a physical transformation like this suddenly calls into question a lot of the reassuring principles you have come to rely on. If this man can suddenly change in this way, maybe other people can, too.

As we will see in the next chapter, preschool children are likely to react as though what they are seeing on television is real. Understanding how profoundly a character transformation violates the preschooler's sense of security may help to explain the intensity of these responses.

The Return of the Hulk—and His Many Cousins

When I started working on this book I thought *The Incredible Hulk* would be useful merely as a historical example to illustrate what a transformation is and to show how a popular program that was based on a transformation had such a powerful effect on young children. But since then, I have discovered that the Hulk is back. Reruns of this program are now being shown during daytime hours on the Sci-Fi Channel, which is part of basic service on many cable systems. So today's children are likely to have the same reactions that occurred almost a generation ago.

But, of course, the Hulk is not alone. Transformations are a staple of scary movies, and we now know a bit more about why they are so upsetting to young children. Animated adventure features are full of transformations: As we saw in chapter 3, *Snow White*'s evil queen becomes the wicked witch, and normal trees turn into grasping monsters. I have received reports of children being especially frightened when the evil Jafar in *Aladdin* suddenly transforms into a vicious cobra, and when naughty little boys in *Pinocchio* grow donkey ears and tails and then bray in panic as they notice what is happening to them.

We also see many scary transformations in popular movies that are not animated. In *The Wizard of Oz,* a particularly frightening scene has Dorothy seeing her beloved auntie Em in the Wicked Witch's crystal ball. Then suddenly, the aunt's reassuring face dissolves into that of the cruelly cackling witch. In *Poltergeist,* a child's dolls and toys that comfortingly surround her during the day turn grotesque and evil as night falls. And then there are those cuddly creatures in *Gremlins,* who suddenly become creepy looking and vicious. The list seems endless.

Many students have reported that Michael Jackson's "Thriller" had especially long-lasting fear effects, in part because of the pop singer's vivid transformation into a werewolf.

> When I was about eight years old my family had dinner at their best friends' house. After dinner at around eight P.M. my parents' friends decided to put on a video. It was the Michael Jackson "Thriller" video. The video turned out to be nothing like I expected. It was about eight minutes long, and from what I remember Michael Jackson was on a date with a girl. He was talking, singing, and dancing. They were in the woods and then all of a sudden his eyes turned yellow and he turned into

a werewolf. The girl ran through the woods to get away from him. Then he was dancing in the streets with a group of people that also had a scary appearance.

That evening I woke up in the middle of the night from a nightmare. I was wrong in thinking that once the video had finished it would be out of my mind forever. I dreamt the vivid images of Michael Jackson turning into a werewolf. I was so terrified to go back to sleep that I woke my mother up. Although she reassured me that it was just a nightmare, I could not get those vivid images out of my mind. For the next few weeks before I went to sleep, the video ran through my head, and some of the nights I had the same nightmare. This video made a lasting impression on me. Even when I see it now, I always get a weird feeling inside of me. I remember the restless nights I sat up thinking about the video.

I have noticed that current scary television programs that are popular with young children, such as *Are You Afraid of the Dark?*, also use the transformation quite heavily. A show I recently watched was about a witch who maintained her outwardly beautiful appearance by tricking young girls, with the promise of eternal beauty, into drinking a potion that transformed them into dogs. The witch's beauty was maintained by cutting out the tongues of the newly transformed dogs and eating them. (No kidding!) At the end, when one skeptical young girl discovers the witch's secret and sends her back to her real appearance

by breaking her magic mirror, we witness the entire transformation of the beautiful woman into a shrieking
thousand-year-old hag, and then finally into a skeleton.
Not an easy image to take at any age!

Once in a while, a transformation goes from the grotesque to the beautiful, as happens at the end of Disney's
Beauty and the Beast. When Belle's love releases the evil
curse on the Beast, we see his various parts gradually
change into those of a handsome young man. While these
transformations can also be unsettling for young children,
clearly the most frightening transformations are the more
common ones that involve the metamorphosis of an attractive, harmless-looking character into a gruesome, grotesque one. This is very understandable, given what we
learned in the last chapter about young children's over-
response to grotesque visual images.

In screening programs for your young child, then, be
especially on the lookout for transformations—no matter
how absurd they may seem from your standpoint. Remember, your child sees things very differently, and as I'll
explain in the next chapter, for very young children, the
images they are seeing are not only disturbing, what they
are seeing is *real.*

CHAPTER FIVE

"But It's Only Make-Believe"

Fantasy, Fiction, and Fear

An example that I will never forget is when I watched the movie Pinocchio. *I saw this movie with my mother when I was about four or five years old. I really thought that what was happening in the movie was real. In the movie, if a child misbehaved, he or she was turned into a donkey. Also, if a child lied, their nose would grow. I really believed that this would happen to me if I was bad. I remember being extremely scared even a few weeks after I had seen the movie because I thought that the same thing would happen to me if I misbehaved.*

This description serves as a vivid reminder that children often fully believe stories that we adults are quick to dismiss as fantastic or impossible. Developmental psychologists have noted that children only gradually come to understand the difference between reality and fantasy. And children learn to say that some things are real and others are make-believe long before they understand what it means to be make-believe. They will tell you that *Peter Pan*'s Captain Hook is make-believe long before they stop worrying that he will capture them and feed them to the crocodile! This lack of understanding plays a key role in the things that frighten young children. Until children understand that something that is not real cannot pose a threat, they will be just as scared by TV shows and movies portraying fantasy outcomes as by those portraying real dangers. Indeed, often the young child will be more frightened by fantasy characters, because fantasy villains are usually ugly and grotesque. As children come to understand the distinction between fantasy and reality, they better appreciate that only real threats and dangers can harm them.

Why Learning What's Make-Believe Is So Difficult

As adults, we seem to take the distinction between fantasy and reality for granted. But put yourself in the situation of the very young child, and you will realize that differentiating between what's real and what's make-believe is not an easy task. At first, maybe it does seem simple. The newborn or infant believes what he sees, feels, hears, smells, and tastes to be true—and, for the most part, it generally is. But soon the young child is exposed to things that are beyond his immediate experience. One way in which this happens is through language. Beyond seeing and feeling and hearing a dog, for example, a child can hear someone talk about a dog or have a book about a dog read to him. Through language and pictures, he learns about things that he doesn't experience directly. Over time, he comes to know that everything anyone says isn't necessarily true in the same way that something he witnesses himself is usually true. But it takes a long time to come to this realization.

Although parents often make a concerted effort to teach their children the difference between real and make-believe, we also have a few customs that undermine these efforts. Most parents make it a point to communicate the value of telling the truth, especially within the family. And yet most of us promote elaborate stories about Santa Claus, the tooth fairy, or the Easter Bunny. I'm not saying that the enjoyment of these cultural myths is inappropriate or wrong, but it does complicate the child's task of sorting out what's real and what's make-believe.

Piaget's take on this situation was to say that preschool, or preoperational, children do not distinguish play and reality as two distinct realms with different ground rules. My own family brought this issue home, so to speak, one Christmas a few years ago. We were visiting my husband's relatives, and as in millions of other families, all the young children hung their stockings on the mantel, leaving milk and cookies for Santa Claus. And like many parents, the adults warned the children to go right to bed because Santa wouldn't want to see them awake when he came to deliver their presents. By morning, of course, Santa had left presents and even drunk the milk and eaten one of the cookies. When the children were applauded for having gone right to sleep, one bright four-year-old among them replied, "I saw Santa last night! I stayed up and watched him, but he didn't see me!"

Now, how can you argue with a response like that? Was he telling an out-and-out lie? If so, he could hardly be blamed for imitating his parents' attitude toward the truth. Was he talking about a dream he had that he thought was true? Or was he playing by the ground rules he observed regarding Santa Claus? We'll never know for sure because we adults were too embarrassed to question him. But this incident illustrates one of the ways in which the border between what's real and what's make-believe becomes fuzzy.

Reality vs. Fantasy

Television is another factor that makes the distinction between fantasy and reality especially complicated. Many of the images on television and in movies are so similar to real life that it is tempting to believe, at first, that what is shown there is real. It takes a very long time for children to sort out this paradox.

The distinction, for television, is not simply one of "real" vs. "pretend." Children must learn many variations of the difference between real and make-believe. At first children believe that the things they are seeing are actually inside the television set—that if they look inside, they'll find those things and that what's in there might actually be able to come out. Research suggests that by about the age of four or so, they understand that the things they are seeing are not actually in the box, but that is just the first step toward understanding television's many realities.

By about the age of seven or eight, according to research, children come to distinguish between things that are real and those that are make-believe on television. At first they judge what is make-believe by its format, concluding that all cartoons are make-believe and all live-action shows are real. But over time, they become conscious of the fact that certain things that they see in fantasy shows are physically impossible, whether they are shown through animation or live action. They understand, for example, that people don't fly the way Peter Pan and Superman do on television and in movies. They come to judge whether something on television is real on the basis of whether the things they see in a story actually exist in the real world. A police story is real, they will say, because there are police in the real world, but stories with certain types of villains, such as witches and monsters, are not real because these characters are not found in real life.

And how do children learn to distinguish between people, animals, and events that exist in the real world and those that do not? Surprisingly, there's no simple rule.

Children just have to learn this by experience. There is no obvious distinguishing characteristic for what is plausible and what is fantastic. What is it about dragons that causes them to be make-believe, while dinosaurs are real? There's nothing in the way they look in pictures that could tip a child off. There are many things that are real that seem downright outrageous when you think about them: the fact that the pictures you see on television can come to your home invisibly through the air or the fact that planes can fly or, for that matter, the way babies are made. None of these ideas seems very realistic on the surface. Over time, we come to accept some very weird things as real, while we learn that other things are impossible. It's no wonder that children take a long time to understand what can and cannot happen.

In choosing programs for preschool children, then, you should not be reassured when a story contains scary elements that are physically impossible, such as a prince turning into a frog, a sorcerer casting evil spells, or a monster devouring a city. These outlandish happenings will not make the story any less compelling or frightening. Focus your attention on the elements of the story that were discussed in the previous two chapters: Are there dangerous-looking animals or grotesque characters? Do they make intense and disturbing sounds or threaten physical harm? Do normal-looking beings transform into hideous monsters?

Similarly, with realistic shows, what you need to look

for when screening them for preschoolers is how disturbing they are in terms of these surface features, not whether they present realistic threats. By the time children reach the age of eight or so, however, it will matter to them whether programs are based on reality or not, and the real ones will be scarier.

Research confirms that as children get older, they become less and less scared by fantasy programs and movies, but they continue to be frightened—and sometimes become *more* frightened—by realistic portrayals. In the survey we conducted in the early eighties, in which we asked parents of children from kindergarten through fourth grade which programs and movies had frightened their child, we categorized the content as either fantasy (showing impossible events, as in *The Wizard of Oz*) or fiction (showing things that could possibly occur, as in *Jaws*). In the parents' responses, mentions of fantasy fare decreased as the child's age increased, and mentions of fictional offerings actually increased with age. Our more recent survey of parents of children in kindergarten, second, fourth, and sixth grade reconfirmed the importance of the fantasy-reality distinction in what frightens children. Although children in all grades were scared by such realistic offerings as *Rescue 911*, only children in the younger two groups had problems with such obviously fantastic offerings as *Peter Pan, Batman,* and *The Wizard of Oz*. When children themselves name the TV shows and movies that frighten them, we see the same trends. Evil witches and monsters recede in the nightmares of older elementary-school children and are replaced by dangerous animals and vicious criminals. The following two examples are typical of what frightens this older group:

One night my Girl Scout troop had a slumber party. We all got ready for bed in our sleeping bags in front of the TV and watched Creepshow. *It was a collection of short thrillers. Some were stupid, and a couple have stuck with me the rest of my life. One short story was about a man in his apartment. He had a few cockroaches; then they started to multiply. They were coming out of the drains and out of the light fixtures. Eventually they overwhelmed the man and killed him. They were all over him coming out of his nose and mouth. I believe that I have more than normal feelings of disgust when it comes to all sorts of bugs. It could be due to seeing these past images. Even today I can't sleep unless my mouth is shut. Who knows, a bug could crawl in when I was sleeping.*

One of the few television programs that I can still clearly remember as having frightened me for a long time was the show Hunter. *I was probably nine or ten years old at the time and my older brother was baby-sitting. He wanted to watch it, so I remember sitting down to watch it with him. It was an episode about a man who would kidnap little girls and then bury them alive. He had killed a number of them already when the show started and the two police detectives on the show caught him just as he was about to bury another one. They had already found the bodies of a few of the others. This was the first time that I had ever seen kidnapping on television or anywhere for that matter. I was scared for many nights after seeing the program that I would be kidnapped and buried alive by some psychopath.*

Fiction: That Frightening Middle Ground

According to research, children by about the age of ten come to grasp more than simply what's possible and impossible in the media. They come to appreciate that some programs are scripted and acted for the purpose of telling a story. Before that time, they are likely to think that a family drama shows the real activities of a real family and that a realistic adventure story shows events that actually transpired.

Once children know that dramas and comedies contain actors speaking lines that were written for them, does this knowledge prevent them from being unduly scared by most entertainment offerings? If only this were the case! Unfortunately, fiction can be very scary.

When children come to understand that most programs and almost all movies are scripted and performed by actors, they at first think that all scripted stories are untrue. But over time, they learn that there is an important category between the programs that show real events that actually happened (such as the news and documentaries) and fantasies, which portray unreal, impossible events that could never happen in the real world. That intermediate category is fiction, which is the product of someone's imagination but is based on events that can and do occur.

There are several reasons why we respond so intensely to television shows and movies, even when we know that what we're seeing is fiction. First of all, we automatically fear certain dangerous things in real life, and we have an immediate fear reaction even when we see these things on the screen. Over time, and as we grow older, we may still have that initial reaction, but it is less intense as we distinguish between the scary things that are really present and can harm us and those that are only being represented to us on video or in film. We are also naturally inclined to empathize with other people's emotions, and as we become attached to characters in a movie, we often feel emotions similar to the ones they are feeling. Again, we can keep reminding ourselves that these are not real people, but for many of us, our emotions become strongly intertwined with those of the characters we view, and we sometimes care deeply about what happens to them. We also watch TV and movies for entertainment, and often we purposely throw ourselves into the story, adopting an attitude that is sometimes referred to as "the willing suspension of disbelief."

As adults, though, it seems that we ought to be able to leave our emotions in the theater after the movie is over. Even if we cared about the fictional heroine who was stalked by the psychopathic killer, we should not still be worrying days later if we saw her escape unharmed, should we? But we often continue to feel anxious, and for good reason. Because fiction is based on things that can and do happen, watching a scary program heightens our fears of real events like those in the program. A fictional story about the kidnapping of a young child may be entirely made up by the dramatist, and yet the elements of the story are real. Watching a program about a kidnapped young child intensifies our awareness of this risk. If we feel that it could happen to us (or our child) we will feel more threatened by that possibility, and this feeling of vulnerability is likely to last as long as our memory of the program. The more a fictionalized threat is similar to things that threaten us in our own lives, the more scared we will be, not just while watching, but afterward as well. This applies to children, too.

After the movie *Jaws* came out, it was children at the beach who suffered the most obvious spillover effects. I have received dozens of reports of ruined seaside vacations:

> When the film Jaws *arrived at the movie theaters, everyone considered it a "must-see" movie. Naturally, my friends and I attended this feature. This was the first "scary" movie my parents had allowed me to see. While I was quite aware of the immediate fright reaction induced by viewing this movie, I was naive to the possibility of any long-term or lingering effects.*

About a year later, a vacation to the Florida coast caused the dreaded sensation to resurface. As we approached the shoreline, an alarm rifled through my body. I knew Jaws was circling just beyond the swimming markers. Consequently, I refused to enter the water. Subsequent vacations have yielded the same reaction. I think I was the only person in Hawaii who would not step into the ocean. I considered the surfers suicidal maniacs. Weren't they aware of the eminent risks?

It also seems that young girls just starting out on their baby-sitting careers were the most frightened by the movie *When a Stranger Calls,* which showed a baby-sitter being stalked by a psychopathic killer. The *Friday the Thirteenth* series did not make it any easier for teenagers going camping. The list goes on. You don't have to believe that any of these specific events ever really happened to feel threatened when engaging in activities similar to those of the victims in these movies. These movies heighten our awareness of dreadful possibilities.

When I was in (about) the third grade my friends and I had a slumber party, and we decided to watch a horror movie. In this movie a group of teenage girls were having a slumber party, and one by one throughout the movie they disappeared and were gruesomely murdered. The movie showed explicit details of their deaths, and one aspect that particularly affected me were the scenes of them pleading for their lives. I remember seeing the terror in their eyes as they begged to be spared, and I remember hoping each time that they would get away, and how awful I felt when they were murdered anyway. That night none of us could sleep, and every sound that we heard scared all of us to a point where we would scream, and we eventually ended up huddled together for the entire night to protect each other. We were so scared that none of us would even get up and go to the bathroom. Even after that night the images of the young girls begging for mercy stuck in my head. For many nights after that I had nightmares and difficulty sleeping, every sound I heard scared me, and I thought that some killer was coming to get me.

Children who find themselves in the same situation as the fictional victim become especially frightened by a plot that makes them acutely aware of what might happen to them. But scary programs do more than that. These movies contain all sorts of devices that engage our emotions more strongly than a simple reminder about possible risks. Scary movies and TV shows include a variety of elements that usually are not there when we face real threats in our own lives.

First, there's suspense. In the real world, when a vicious attack, major tragedy, or accident occurs, we usually have no forewarning. These things often happen very quickly, before the victim even realizes what is happening.

However, the television or movie producer rarely lets things occur that way. Most scary programs and movies let us know what is going to happen or what might happen, and we become anxious well in advance of the horrifying outcome. Research shows that it's much more frightening this way. Because these shows are meant to be scary, the producer dramatizes the events to evoke the most intense emotions from the audience.

> *The movie was* Friday the Thirteenth. *This particular movie was very uncomfortable because it was suspense-filled. The reason I was scared was because I knew the people were going to die, yet I did not know the exact moment it was going to happen. The actual horror of the movie did not scare me (ex.: blood, people having their heads cut off). But when I was unable to know when the person was going to be killed, or where the killer Jason was, this is what bothered me.*

Another element of frightening films that is absent when real threats occur is the musical score and other sound effects. It seems that music and sound effects dramatically affect our emotional reactions. Sudden loud noises shock and arouse us, and we automatically respond with fear to the shrieks and cries of victims.

Many retrospective reports of movie-induced fright refer to the power of sound effects and music. Here are a few examples:

. . . And the suspenseful music that accompanied the shark attacks is forever imprinted in my mind. I just have to play the [Jaws] music in my head when I'm swimming and I can really scare myself.

In the movie [Friday the Thirteenth] the sound was high and loud, and the music was scary. While I was watching the movie, I knew I did not like the music and the sound because it was the signal of killing. Every time I heard this kind of sound, I would know that more people would be killed, and they could not do anything to protect themselves.

One particular scene from the movie [Piranha] that had a great effect on me took place at a summer camp for kids. The children in the scene were participating in various summertime activities, including swimming in the lake. There were underwater camera shots of the swimmers' feet and of the killer fish approaching for the attack. Along with these shots were terrible spine-chilling sound effects supposedly coming from the fish and a scary type of music used to create suspense. At the moment of the attack people were screaming and frantically swimming to escape from the killer fish.

By using these dramatic devices, movies and TV shows aim to intensify our response and etch the scary scenes indelibly in our minds in a way that many real events do not.

Remember, most vicious and brutal attacks are not witnessed by anyone; even the victim may be taken by surprise. Loved ones of the victim usually only hear about the attack and are left to imagine what it must have been like. But television and movies enact these attacks in lurid detail, exposing us to horrid scenes we might never experience in our entire lives. These images will be especially riveting for children and teenagers, who have less experience with such fictional stories and a less mature understanding of how movies and TV programs use special features to manipulate their emotions. Because these elements are so vivid, children are especially susceptible to their terror-intensifying effects.

The Vulnerable Female

If there is any fictional theme that repeats and repeats itself in the horror stories I receive from college students, it's the theme of the violent victimization of young women, usually by men. Often the theme involves sexual assault, and as you would expect, the most intense reactions to these plots come from female viewers. Content analyses have shown that in horror movies, attacks against men are usually over and done with quickly, but attacks against women are longer and more drawn out, making the viewer see the female victims suffer more and show more fear. This is one theme that has an intense impact not only on young teenage girls but on women in college as well. The following example is typical:

The action that sparked my fear response was a violent, very graphic portrayal of an attempted rape with a young girl as the victim. The scene used fast cutting, close-ups, suspenseful music, and the sound of the girl crying to aid in its intensity. During the entire scene I felt tense. It was as though I didn't notice the other things around me. I was truly frightened. I experienced empathy for the victim and uncomfortable thoughts that these acts occur every day in the real world. I tried to imagine what must have been running through the young girl's head. All I could say over and over again was "That's so horrible, how awful!" The imagery of the rape scene seemed to haunt me as I sat down to begin studying. I couldn't get the scene out of my head.

This description shows that the woman who wrote it had an awareness of the various production techniques that were used to intensify her response. But she was also aware of the importance of the theme of female victimization:

The intensity of my response has to do with my close identification with the subject matter at hand. Forced sexual acts are a major concern and fear of many women in the real world. My fear response was more intense in this case because I could relate to and identify with the underlying implications of the scene. To me this was not a random act of violence; it was an issue that hit close to home.

The fact that television dramas and movies play on women's fears of victimization comes up over and over again in women's memories of their media traumas. For example:

One of the scariest things I have ever seen was on Beverly Hills, 90210 *sophomore year in college. Now, I know that this sounds like the silliest thing that you have ever heard—a twenty-year-old girl being afraid of a show as bad as* 90210, *but it is true. Let me explain. Two years ago there was a plot about Donna and a stalker. Being that she was the only virgin on the show, this news was particularly surprising. Anyway, the point is that the whole episode that week revolved around this guy breaking into Donna's beautiful beachfront apartment, sneaking around in the dark, and then getting very close to raping her. Obviously, he did not get the chance to rape her since Donna's boyfriend, David, arrived in the nick of time. But he got pretty damn close—way too close for my comfort. This somewhat-normal-appearing man was walking around in her apartment with a crowbar waiting for her to come into her room on a night that he knew she was all alone. Granted, I was sitting in a room with the five other girls I lived with, but they were still all girls and at some point I knew I would be alone in the apartment.*

Now this was not the most frightening experience I have ever had, but it has stuck with me. When I am walking alone at night sometimes or I am in the house by

myself, I am that little bit more nervous. I am no lu-
natic; I just have memories of that episode and wonder
what would happen if my David did not come to the
door at that precise moment.

The prevalence of the theme of sexual assault in young women's traumatic responses to fictional programs and movies is striking. Maybe it is due to the fact that all women are potential victims of sexual assault; in fictional plots women do not have to be involved in risky activities to become a victim. In contrast, it seems that men who are victims in fiction are typically involved in activities that make violence more likely: They are criminals, police officers, vigilantes, or soldiers. Truly random assaults seem much more rare for the male fictional character. Of course it's true that women are more vulnerable than men to sexual assault in real life, but many movies and television programs play on this fear to an extent that can cause obsessive fear reactions, particularly among younger girls who are not well equipped to put the disturbing images in context.

The Supernatural: The Gray Area between Fantasy and Fiction

A second theme that comes up over and over again in the media-induced fears of older elementary-school children and teenagers is that of the supernatural and the occult. This area is hard to define because it seems to occupy the border between fantasy and fiction. As I said earlier, by the time children reach the age of seven or eight, they are aware that certain fantasy happenings are impossible. However, many people never seem to fully reject the possibility of such supernatural events as alien attacks and demonic possession. *The Exorcist* is a film about demonic possession that has powerful effects, even on adults. Similarly, a film like *Poltergeist,* which shows supernatural attacks on a family whose house was built over a graveyard, plays on viewers' superstitions and the ambiguous lines between what's possible and impossible. Many movies and programs play on that ambiguity. In addition, they often contain elements of real threats that even the most skeptical adults can fear. Michael Myers, the homicidal maniac in *Halloween,* keeps coming back from the dead. As adults, we know that can't happen. However, we do know that homicidal maniacs exist, so we can still feel vulnerable even if we don't believe that aspect of the plot.

Stories of the supernatural defy the reassuring laws of physics that adults and older children rely on in evaluating risks. For example, it does no good to lock all the doors if the villain can penetrate the walls. Supernatural plots are much less predictable. The older child cannot rely on his knowledge of what is real and what is make-believe. Anything can happen.

I've suffered from nightmares after watching Aliens *(around the age of twelve). The creatures themselves are what scared me: both their gruesome appearance and their apparent intelligence. In the movie they outsmart the humans, who are no match for the aliens, even with their weapons. My room makes strange sounds at night (at least I perceive strange sounds in my room, particularly in my attic). In one scene from the movie, the humans could tell the aliens were near but had no idea where they were. It turned out the aliens were directly above them, in the ceiling. Lying awake in my bed, I could hear odd noises coming (seemingly) from my attic right above me, and I imagined an alien shifting around up there. The situation where the aliens were above the humans and came through the ceiling created an image of the same thing happening in my room. This occurred pretty frequently for about a month after viewing the movie. A couple times I even had nightmares about the creatures.*

Another problem is that the credibility of occult happenings is reinforced by frequent reports of unexplained supernatural events in reality-based programs:

The film I viewed was The Exorcist. *It contained graphic scenes of a young girl possessed by the devil. I was approximately twelve years old at the time and was in a slumber-party situation. I vividly remember the stress this film caused me. I was not only extremely afraid of the devil and evil, but I became obsessed with the possibility of becoming possessed myself. To make matters worse, later on in the same week I came home from school and turned on some afternoon talk show with the subject matter consisting of "real" stories of "real" people who were at one time possessed. That program and the movie were enough to keep me from sleeping for two nights straight and finally when I did fall asleep I had terrible nightmares. I slept with my parents for the next few weeks.*

Just as parents sometimes make it harder for preschoolers to distinguish fantasy and reality by promoting the tooth fairy, our mass media make the distinction more ambiguous for all of us by overplaying the credibility of supernatural forces. By the teen years, most kids have learned that certain things can't happen, but can they be absolutely sure? And, they might well wonder, what if they're wrong?

We turn next to a domain where there's no ambiguity about real vs. make-believe: the news and other reports of real events that actually happened.

CHAPTER **SIX**

When Reality Is a Nightmare

All the News That's Fit to Terrify

When I was about eleven years old I saw something on television that scared me enough to make me remember it vividly all of these years. It wasn't a scary movie but a newsclip of something that really happened. A young, oriental man was being held in handcuffs by two men in uniforms (of some sort). I cannot recall the greatest detail about them because that is not what has stuck in my mind all this time. It was the young fellow I cannot forget about. As he was being restrained, he looked very frightened and powerless. At the mercy of these two men, it was obvious he had no escape. Then I saw a gun go up to his temple. My mouth fell open as I thought, "They can't just shoot him!" But I was wrong. Ten seconds later a shot rang through the air and the man fell to the ground, with blood spurting out of his head. His body

*lay lifeless. I sat there not being able to believe what I had
just seen. . . . Luckily I haven't seen many of these types
of scenes on television, but the one I did see will remain
in my memory forever.*

How many other children were devastated by this infamous news moment during the Vietnam War? And how many more graphic incidents like that one are our children being exposed to these days? Think of the many recent upsetting stories that have been covered heavily by television news: the Rodney King beating, the Oklahoma City bombing, the shooting deaths of children at school, innumerable natural disasters, and countless stories of child molestation and murder—this list could go on and on. There is little doubt that television news is becoming more graphic and sensational. A recent study reported that local news is especially violent. Of one hundred newscasts analyzed on a single day, the average "mayhem index" was 43 percent, meaning almost half of the news in the program involved violence or disasters.

What children see on news shows really frightens them. In the survey we did in the early eighties, in which we asked parents to name the television shows and movies that had frightened their child, television news stories were in the top ten in terms of the number of parents who mentioned them. The most frequently cited news story at that time was the Atlanta child murders case, in which a serial killer repeatedly targeted young children.

A decade later, shortly after the war in the Persian Gulf, almost half of a random sample of parents my colleagues and I contacted said their child had been upset by television coverage of the war.

Age Trends in News Stories That Frighten

More recently, in the random survey of parents with children in kindergarten through sixth grade that we did in the spring of 1994, we found that 37 percent said their child had been frightened or upset by a television news story during the preceding year. In this study, we were looking for age trends in what had frightened them.

Our first expectation was that the news would become more frightening as children got older because of their emerging appreciation for the reality-fantasy distinction. As children come to know that fantasy dangers cannot harm them but real dangers can, they can become more and more attuned to the threats that television news consistently depicts. Our survey showed this to be true. There was an upward trend in the percentage of children frightened by the news, going from 26 percent of the kindergartners to 44 percent of the sixth graders. We observed the greatest increase in the scariness of news between kindergarten and second grade. You may remember that this is approximately the same time that children are becoming competent in making the distinction between fantasy and reality.

What types of news stories frightened children the most? More than one-third of the children who had been frightened by the news were scared by stories portraying criminal violence, such as shootings, muggings, and kidnappings. Almost as many children were frightened by stories about foreign wars and famine, of which there were many during the period of the survey, particularly from Bosnia, Rwanda, and Somalia.

One-fourth of the children frightened by news were scared by stories about natural disasters. Again, there were many disasters in the news during that time, including severe earthquakes and rampaging fires in California, as well as devastating floods, hurricanes, and tornadoes around the country.

Children were especially responsive to stories in which a child was the victim. Many of them explicitly told their parents that they were afraid that what they saw in the news story would happen to them, too. Girls were especially likely to be upset after viewing the victimization of children.

We also found differences in the kinds of news stories that frightened children at different ages: Older children were much more responsive than younger children to crime stories featuring violence, but younger children were a great deal more upset than older children by news coverage of natural disasters.

Why these age differences? It seems to me that these differences are in line with what we have observed regarding younger children's responsiveness to visual images.

When you think about it, news stories featuring criminal violence are usually not that explicitly visual. Rarely are crimes of violence caught on camera. When they are, as in the Rodney King beating, I would expect younger children to be as frightened by them as older children. But the typical crime story shows only the aftermath of violence, which usually is not as visually vivid as the crime itself. The most upsetting part of many crime stories, particularly when the crime is between strangers, is the notion of the viewer's own vulnerability, rather than the crime itself.

Natural disasters, in contrast, are usually dramatically visual, and television news stresses the images of devastation: Homes are shown being ripped apart by hurricanes, swept away in floods, or crushed in earthquakes, and this footage is frequently accompanied by images of frightened bystanders or sobbing victims. These events are easy for children to understand. The images are readily remembered and often cause children to worry that a similar disaster will happen to them next.

There are some trends in children's fears in general that are helpful in predicting the types of news stories that will frighten children of different ages. Dozens of studies have been conducted in which children have been asked what frightens them, and there is a large consensus regarding age trends in fears.

The research suggests that three- to eight-year-olds are most often frightened by animals; the dark; supernatural

beings, such as ghosts, monsters, and witches; and by anything that looks strange or moves suddenly. These findings
are very consistent with what we have observed about children's reactions to fantasy programming, but of course
these things rarely appear in the news. In contrast, the fears
of nine- to twelve-year-olds most often relate to personal injury and physical destruction. This category includes accidents, kidnapping, disease, and violence—the essential
focus of much television news. Teenagers continue to fear
personal injury, but in addition, they begin to have fears
related to more abstract issues such as economic problems, global disharmony, and environmental devastation. It
should be helpful to keep these trends in mind when determining which news stories may frighten your child.

Getting the Message Out

I had been working on this book for some time when I
suddenly recognized the importance of spreading the information about children's reactions to news. I received a
distress call from a mother on the East Coast who reported
that her daughter's school had adopted the policy of
showing the children news excerpts every morning. Her
child, a ten-year-old, had had an intense fright reaction to
the coverage of the murder of JonBenet Ramsey (the
kindergarten beauty queen who was found dead in the
basement of her own home). At my request, the mother
wrote down and sent me her account of what her daughter had said:

"Mom, you won't believe what was on the news today! This girl was killed in her own house, Mom. In her own house! I'm sorry, Mom, but I am not going to be able to be by myself in the house ever again even in my room, and I am never going in the basement alone anymore. And you know, they showed her funeral. I never even knew her and I felt like I was at her funeral. That is something private, Mom. I shouldn't have been there. I didn't even know her and I was at her funeral."

It is not difficult to understand why children often have such intense reactions to television news. It's very normal to feel sorry and sad for a real victim who suffered a real tragedy, but more than empathy is fueling children's intense reactions. After all, the news displays many horrible things that not only *can* happen—they *did* happen. Obviously, if something did happen, it can happen again.

This possibility may provoke lasting fears:

A [television] crew was interviewing a woman when her estranged husband suddenly jumped into the picture and shot her several times. The image of this crazed man ruthlessly gunning down the woman is permanently burned into my mind. . . . I guess, in a way, that image made me lose a little trust in the people that are closest to me. It makes me think that people could snap in an instant.

If It Bleeds, It Leads

These findings on children's emotional disturbances raise the question: How much news should parents allow their children to see? Many parents who restrict entertainment fare are reluctant to limit exposure to news on the grounds that news is educational. Many television news producers respond to criticism of their policy of always choosing a bloody incident as the lead story by saying that their critics are advocating censorship. They argue that the bloody incident is there because it happened and that not to show it would infringe upon our right to know.

What these arguments ignore, of course, is that whatever makes it onto television news is there because someone decided it was newsworthy. Thousands of things happen every day that could be on the news, but only a few events can be chosen. We must remember that one primary function of television news is to sell commercial spots to advertisers. Therefore, the news must be programmed to ensure that a large audience will tune in. To be news, a story has to be different or unusual. Most planes don't crash, so a routine flight doesn't make the news, but when a crash occurs, we always hear about it. What many news programmers believe is that sensational news is what draws people to watch, and as we'll discuss in more detail in chapter 9, to some extent they are right. There is a big audience for news about violent incidents and criminal behavior.

The temptation to be sensational is strongest for television, because television puts the highest value on striking visual images. An unimportant incident that has arresting videotape has a better chance to make it onto television than something more important that is too abstract to photograph. And, as we've seen, sensational visuals are especially problematic for our youngest children.

Those Popular Police, Crime, and Rescue Shows

As if the news weren't enough, television provides us with many more opportunities to witness the horror and tragedy of violent incidents that are real. We are currently in an era in which reality-based shows such as *Rescue 911* and *Cops* and documentaries about crime and other dangers are quite popular and readily available in the early evening when many children are in the audience.

In our most recent random survey of parents, *Rescue 911* was mentioned more often than any other program (including fantasy and fiction genres) as causing fear in children. Remember the anecdotes from chapter 1 about the child who quit skiing and the child who gave up cooking as a result of watching this program? I personally observed the effect of *Rescue 911* a few years ago when my son had his slightly older friend sleep over. Although this friend had previously been a good role model for going to bed without fear, that night he repeatedly ran into our bedroom, saying he thought burglars were trying to get in the window. Since this was so different from his usual behavior, I asked his mother the next day if she had noticed her son having trouble sleeping. She replied that she had, and that the problem started when he began watching *Rescue 911.*

The program, it turns out, touts itself as having an educational focus: In addition to showing near misses to serious tragedies, it does give tips on how to avoid them. Unfortunately, for many children, the brief safety instructions do little to undo the alarming effects of watching the life-threatening incidents.

Unsolved Mysteries is another good example of a well-intentioned program that scares kids anyway. Not only does this program provide children with vivid re-creations of crimes that actually happened, but the fact that the perpetrators are still on the loose makes children feel even more vulnerable. Here's a good example of what I mean:

> *The only frightening experience that I can recall happened while I was watching* Unsolved Mysteries *when I was in high school. The mystery was about a teenage girl in Texas who was abducted from a car wash in the summer at dusk. At the time she had been missing six months. On the show they did a reenactment of what may have happened to her and this is the part I remember the most vividly. They showed the girl leaving her house and telling her parents that she is going to the car wash. She drives there; the car wash is one of those self-*

clean ones and it looks as though it was in the middle of nowhere. It is in a rural area and there are no other people around. So, she begins to wash her car, and another car pulls up, a bearded, middle-age man gets out, grabs her, they struggle, and she is taken. Her car door's left open, radio on, with her money and identification left in the car. Her parents were the last people to see her. I think I remember this because I live in a rural area and when I go there I drive past a car wash similar to that one. I never questioned my safety there at any time until this story. I often wonder what happened to her.

Documentaries can have the same devastating effect:

As a child of about ten, I watched a television show about missing children. I saw little girls who looked just like me, that had been taken from their parents. I remember imagining all the terrible things that strangers were probably doing to the children. I remember curling up into a ball and crying for these children; yet I was still unable to call for my mom. I needed to know what happened to all of the children, if any had been rescued. I realized the same thing could happen to me. I was terrified that I would be taken from my mom. I was afraid to go anywhere alone. I could not be in the basement anymore, which was where I originally saw the show. If I had to go into the basement, I would run as fast as I could downstairs and then back up. It seems as though

from that night on I knew someone was going to kidnap
me. At bedtime, I would try to camouflage myself on the
bed so they would not know I was there. Many nights I
crept into my parents' bed to feel safe. My reaction to the
show gradually disappeared over the next year.

Making Wise News Choices for Children

Let's return to the story of the mother who contacted me
about her daughter's reaction to seeing the JonBenet
Ramsey murder coverage at school. The reason the mother
called me was to enlist my help in convincing the school
to be more careful in selecting news stories to present to
ten-year-olds. At first, the child's teachers did not seem to
be responsive to the mother's request that the news be
screened in advance. But after I sent her some reprints of
the research cited in this chapter, she and her husband
got the school to modify its policy. The teachers now
watch the news before showing it to the children, and
leave out the most violent and sensational stories, particularly those involving child victims. It is to the school's
credit that they were willing to modify their policies to ac-
commodate the emotional needs of their students when
relevant research findings were brought to their attention.

I am not advocating censorship, and I don't think that
children should be brought up to believe that the real
world is nothing but sweetness and light. But I consider
it fully legitimate to ask whether children shouldn't be
shielded from the TV-news version of reality, which pre-

sents much more horrifying images of the world than they would otherwise experience. At what age should we burden children with such graphic, often gory images as victims of bombings, molestation, and murder; terminally ill AIDS patients; and parents sobbing over the deaths of their children in accidents? In my opinion, we needn't be in any rush.

Children need, of course, to be informed about specific threats to their safety. They also need to be introduced to the negative aspects of the world around them. But much of that information should be presented in small and less-threatening doses, not in the sensational fashion that television news typically employs.

My advice to parents with regard to television news and reality programming is, Beware! The nightly news is full of graphic visual images of death and destruction, and television has recently adopted a special fascination with the theme of children as victims. Children may not be interested in the news, but they will be affected by it if you watch it when they're around. If you have preschool children, the safest bet is to watch the news when they are in bed or get your news from the papers. For older elementary-school children you might watch a station with a family-friendly news broadcast if there's one in your area.

As your children reach their teens and are ready to grapple with these difficult issues, I would keep tabs on the news they are watching and be ready to discuss it with them. (See chapter 8 for advice on these discussions.)

CHAPTER SEVEN

When Words Won't Work

How to Help a Frightened Preschooler

When I was five years old, I was very scared after watching the movie The Wizard of Oz. *I was terrified of the Wicked Witch of the West. I thought she was hiding in my closet or under my bed; I figured that sooner or later she would jump out and say, "I'll get you, my pretty!" and send the flying monkeys after me. My dad tried to calm me by explaining that there were no witches; furthermore, there wasn't enough room for one under my bed or in my closet. He explained that monkeys can't really fly or hurt little girls; besides, no monkey would be able to get into the house since the doors were locked. Unfortunately, although my father's arguments seem perfectly logical now, they were useless when I was five years old. I was totally unable to grasp the fact that witches were the result of a movie producer's imagination and nothing to be feared. Logical explanations were futile; I still made my dad check my closet and bed for witches be-fore I would go to sleep.*

"You Can Talk Till You're Blue in the Face"

An early study of children and fear tells the story of the young child who sat down and classified fairy-tale characters as "real" or "unreal." It was an ambitious at-tempt to overcome his fear, but it didn't work. He was still scared of them regardless of their category. As we saw in chapter 5, it takes a long time for children to fully under-stand the true meaning of the difference between fantasy and reality. To a very young child, just because something is make-believe, it doesn't mean it can't come and get you in the night!

But many parents think telling a young child that a television story is not real helps their child overcome his fears. When my colleagues and I questioned parents of pre-schoolers in a survey, most of them said they used that type of explanation when coping with their child's TV fears.

The fact is, young children usually don't find such words reassuring. One way my colleagues and I verified this was to conduct an experiment. We took a scene from *The Wizard of Oz* that many children find especially scary: Dorothy is in the tower of the Wicked Witch of the West and the witch tells Dorothy that if she doesn't give up the ruby slippers, she will be dead by the time the hourglass is empty.

We showed this scene to both preschool children and nine- to eleven-year-olds. Before they saw it, some children were told to remember, while watching, that it's just a story that's make-believe, that witches are pretend, and that the witch is just a regular person dressed up in a costume. Other children were not given these instructions.

After watching the scene, the children were asked how they had felt while watching it. Did the remember-it's-not-real instructions help children feel less scared? Not the children in the preschool group. Yet the same instructions did make the older children less fearful.

One thing I find really fascinating is that many children are wiser than their parents in knowing what helps them when they are frightened. When my colleagues and I asked children to indicate how helpful different methods would be in making them feel better if they were scared by something on TV, preschoolers thought "tell yourself it's not real" would be the least effective of all the strategies, while nine- to eleven-year-olds thought it would be far and away the best strategy.

Telling yourself it's not real is one of several widely used fear-reducing strategies that are more effective for older children than for younger ones. These methods, which are based on reasoning, usually involve attempts to help the child view the frightening thing in a different light. I refer to these as "verbal strategies" because they require children to process verbal information. Most verbal strategies are ineffective for young children for two reasons. One reason is related to some of the issues I raised in chapter 3 when I talked about how young children's attention is dominated by visual images and things that are easily perceived. As we saw when studying the effect of visual images, the ability to reason about things that are less obvious is very immature in young children, so the ability to use abstract thoughts to overpower frightening images is very weak.

A mother recently told me about the difficulty she had reassuring her five-year-old son who was frightened by the movie *Ghostbusters*. When she tried to explain that ghosts could not come through walls, he replied, "But you're wrong, Mom. I saw it with my own eyes!" This mother's explanation was powerless against the force of the compelling visual images in the movie.

The other problem with verbal strategies is that they rely on the comprehension of words and sentences. Not only are younger children less familiar with the meanings of individual words; they also are less adept at combining word meanings into an overall understanding of a message. Just as we saw that younger children may focus on part of a visual image and ignore the rest of it, they sometimes respond so strongly to a single word that they miss the rest of the sentence.

Another experiment my colleagues and I conducted is a case in point. The results surprised us—and taught us something about the complexities of communicating with preschoolers. Our initial idea was that if we provided children with accurate and reassuring information about something that seemed scary in a movie, the movie would become less frightening. We used the famous snake-pit encounter in *Raiders of the Lost Ark* as our scary scene. Before watching the scene, children of different ages were shown an educational video that tried to convey the fact that most snakes are actually harmless. In the video, the narrator uses the sentence, "Although a few snakes are poisonous, most of them are not."

We expected the video to reduce older children's fear while watching the movie. We also felt it would probably not help the preschoolers because their visceral reaction to the snakes in the movie would outweigh their ability to benefit from the reassuring information. What we discovered was that when these young children heard the word "poisonous," they effectively ignored the rest of the sentence. That word struck such a responsive chord that the intended meaning of the sentence was lost. And not only was this information not helpful to preschoolers—it actually made them more scared! When confronted by the scary visuals in the movie, these children were apparently more sensitive to the danger of snakes than the other children their age who had not viewed the educational video. Our attempt to make these children feel better had the opposite effect.

This is a very good example of the way well-meaning efforts to reduce fear can backfire. What we've learned from this and other studies is how to create explanations that are more suited to a young child's needs. I'll talk in chapter 8 about making explanations more effective even for preschoolers, but in this chapter I'll focus on the techniques that younger children prefer and the ones that work best for them.

What Comforts Little Ones?—First, a Hug

As you might expect from the preceding discussion, the techniques that work for young children do not involve words or mental acrobatics. Simple strategies involving physical comfort, warmth, and closeness are probably the most effective. The same preschoolers who reported that telling themselves it's not real would be ineffective said that getting something to eat or drink or holding a blanket or cuddly toy would help them the most. And of all the techniques we asked children to rate for effectiveness, the one endorsed by the most children is sitting by mom or dad. Children of all ages like touching, holding on to, or being near a warm, caring adult when they are frightened, and this surely has already been demonstrated by the many accounts in this book of children seeking out their parents or even sleeping with them after seeing a scary movie.

An interesting experiment was recently reported in which preschoolers watched a scary television movie with or without their older sister or brother. The researchers found that more than half of the sibling pairs talked about how scary the program was while watching the movie, and more than a third of the older siblings actively tried to comfort their little sisters and brothers by offering words of reassurance, a hug, or a hand to hold. It is not surprising, then, that children who watched with their older siblings were significantly less frightened and enjoyed the program significantly more than those who watched it alone.

In the absence of other real people, young children often choose favorite blankets and cuddly toys for comfort, warmth, and even protection. Sometimes they do this to an exaggerated degree:

> *I would protect and calm myself by putting every single stuffed animal I owned on top of my bed as I slept; this meant about fifty stuffed animals on top of me.*

What our research suggests is that a glass of water, a hug, and the comforting attention of a parent or caregiver is often helpful, and you're better off simply reassuring your preschool child that nothing bad will happen and getting his mind off the topic than trying to explain the specifics of why he is not in danger. For children at this age, providing them with warmth (literally or figuratively) is the best place to start:

> *A technique I used to cope with my fears was to make hot chocolate with my mother and talk about "happy things."*

Often parents are surprised when their rational explanations are not effective with their preschoolers:

> *My mom claims that one calm warm summer night, she and my father felt like watching a scary film,* Creature from the Black Lagoon. *I must have been about four to five years old, and they figured I would have no problem watching because I was with them. Their rationale was, "Hey, he's with us, so we can explain to him that none of this is real." After maybe the first five minutes of the film, when the creature pops out of the pond, I maniacally began to cry my eyes out, and would not stop until my father turned off the television. Mother tells me that no matter how much they tried to explain to me that what was on TV was make-believe, I was still shaking. Her only option was to stay up with me all night, touching me and singing to me softly.*

On the Family Bed, and Eating Your Troubles Away

You may have noticed that some of the techniques that young children prefer are controversial, and you may worry that they risk producing unwanted side effects. For example, many people argue that if children use food to comfort themselves during stress, these habits may come back to haunt them later in terms of obesity or eating disorders. Obviously, this is not what you would want to happen. A drink or a small snack during an acute anxiety state

should not be repeated endlessly. But the occasional use of
food or drink in this context may be very effective in the
short run. Emotions such as fear are felt more intensely on
an empty stomach, the process of eating may itself be distracting and is often pleasant, and a warm drink may take
the chill off that scary feeling. Of course, efforts should be
made to avoid making unscheduled fear-induced snacks a
regular thing.

What may be even more controversial about what
young children like to do when they're scared is the issue
of sleeping in their parents' bed after a nightmare. Experts differ, sometimes vehemently, on whether this should
ever be allowed. The girl whose intense reaction to *The
Elephant Man* was reported in chapter 3 wanted to sleep
with her parents but was forbidden to do so on the advice
of her pediatrician. This physician went so far as to tell her
parents to leave her to cry alone in her bed so that she
wouldn't become too dependent on them. She reported
that neither she nor her parents slept very much for two
years after the movie, but that her parents rewarded her
for every night she did not wake them up, and she was
eventually able to sleep through the night.

I do not believe that there is a single right or wrong
answer to the question of letting your child sleep with you
after a nightmare. As reports in this book show, children
are joining their parents in bed much more frequently
than most parents are willing to admit. Whether this is a
good idea for your family depends on many things, in-

cluding, of course, whether you think this is acceptable behavior and how it affects your own ability to get a good night's sleep. The risk, of course, is that it may become a habit that is difficult to break.

Although the family-bed issue is a controversial one, it seems clear that ignoring, belittling, or punishing children because of their TV-induced fears is a bad idea. Parents who acknowledge their children's fears and help manage them lay the groundwork for a sense of mutual trust and a closeness that will be of use in a variety of other emotional situations. The young woman who suffered Elephant Man nightmares offered these final thoughts:

> *My parents and I agree that they should not have followed my pediatrician's advice. Having to deal with my fears alone clearly made them worse; in retrospect, my parents wish they had been more comforting, and they told me never to leave my own children unconsoled.*

Cutting Out or Cutting Down the Stimulation

Young children who are scared will often try to get away from what's scaring them. If it's television, they may simply leave the room or turn off the TV. If it's a movie, they might scream to be taken out of the theater. That screaming in the theater serves a purpose—by disturbing other viewers, it forces you to leave the theater whether you want to or not.

Trust your crying child: Do not hesitate to remove your child from the scene (or to remove the scary scene from your child). Sometimes parents wonder whether this is a good idea. They hope that if their child will only stay to see the movie through to its happy ending, the fear will go away, and all will be well. Under certain circumstances this approach may work for older children, but there's a good reason it won't work for preschoolers. Very young children are not adept at putting sequences of scenes together in terms of cause and effect: Their fright response to the evil, grotesque monster will not necessarily be reduced by the knowledge that he was killed at the end. Their vivid visual memory may replay and replay the scary scene, whether or not they see the ending. So your best bet is to limit your child's exposure to the program or movie altogether and get him involved in something else as quickly as possible.

One advantage when dealing with preschoolers in this situation is that they are more easily distracted than older children by participation in other activities. With a smaller brain capacity, it is harder for them to keep those horrid events in mind while at the same time focusing on a new activity. Find something pleasurable and distracting to do as soon as possible, and as long as the child seems happy and comfortable, don't feel the necessity of reminding him of his trauma. In many ways, for the preschooler, out of sight is out of mind; don't hesitate to capitalize on this fact.

Another thing young children sometimes do when watching something scary on TV is to stay in the situation, but reduce their exposure to what's troubling them. Some children cover their eyes and peek through their fingers; some peek around a corner or over a pillow; some cover their ears. What they are doing here is exposing themselves to bits and pieces of the program rather than the whole thing. Research shows that these techniques can actually reduce younger children's fright while viewing scary programs. In some cases these activities simply cut down on the scary sights and sounds children receive. In others, they make them feel that they are more in control.

Gradual Exposure in Manageable Doses

Another technique that often works for younger children is referred to as "desensitization." Visual desensitization involves brief exposures to mild versions of something the child finds frightening. As the child becomes comfortable with the mildest version, he then sees a slightly stronger version, with the intensity continuing to increase gradually and only at the rate he can handle. In the experiment we did with *Raiders of the Lost Ark* we also explored whether we could make the snake scene less frightening by desensitizing children to the visual image of snakes. We created a video that showed a series of snakes—first small ones shown from a distance and then larger ones shot from close range. At first the images of snakes were taken from still photos, but as the video progressed, the snakes were shown moving more and more. Children who saw this video were less frightened by the snake-pit scene from the *Raiders* movie than children who had not been gradually exposed to snake visuals. This technique was effective for preschoolers as well as older elementary-school children. Other researchers have found similar results by allowing children to hold rubber replicas of spiders or showing them real lizards and worms before they saw scary movies involving these creatures.

My colleagues and I have also taken on *The Incredible Hulk,* using segments of a *Mister Rogers' Neighborhood* episode intended to reduce children's fear of the Hulk. After children had seen a video of actor Lou Ferrigno having his Hulk makeup applied—a much slower and more understandable transformation than the one in the program—they were less afraid while watching an *Incredible Hulk* episode.

That's fine for the laboratory, but how can parents perform visual desensitization at home? That depends on what your child was scared by. If it was an animal, there are many nature videos and realistic toys that could allow you to gradually introduce your child to the animal in an unthreatening context. A visit to a zoo or pet shop might allow your child to see the animal live—and harmless. For other frightening things, parents might consider books as a way of desensitizing. There are many picture books on the market to help children get over various fears.

Parents themselves have devised all kinds of methods. One mother reported giving her child control of the remote when he was a little scared but wanted to keep watching a video. He would fast-forward his way through parts of movies he found scary. Over time, though, he got used to those scenes and was able to view them in their entirety. Another mother said her preschooler would leave the room during the scene in *Aladdin* when the evil Jafar turns into a huge snake. The boy would remain within earshot so that he could follow the story. Gradually he began staying in the room for longer periods, and now he doesn't leave at all. Both of these stories are examples of mastering fear through desensitization.

A word of caution: Desensitization should only be used when the child really wants to see a scary program or will be exposed to it anyway. A child who is truly traumatized by a program may not be able to view even small portions of it without getting upset. Attempts to desensitize a child in this situation may well make things worse. In these cases, I would recommend avoiding the program or movie entirely. In some cases this will mean avoiding even the opening credits of the program or promos for the movie.

Magical and Mystical Remedies and Rituals

A final set of techniques that preschoolers like may seem totally irrational to the adult, although they do have their own logic in a child's mind. Here I'm talking about the various self-protective rituals children engage in to make themselves feel less vulnerable, usually when they go to bed.

First, there is the repetitive checking to see that the evil being from the television show is not hiding in the closet, under the bed, or behind the curtains. Then there is the defensive posture taken in the bed: Some children insist on facing the door for protection; others need to have their back to the door. Many children need to sleep with the light or a night-light on. Some children bring weapons of their own to bed just in case (one young man claimed to have slept with his baseball bat for years). And there's also the defensive gear, such as the blanket used to ward off vampires that was mentioned in chapter 1. Children can be very creative in selecting their methods of feeling more secure. I don't see a problem with these devices as long as they don't interfere with the child's (or his roommates') ability to get a healthy night's sleep.

Sometimes magic is invoked:

> *For as long as I can remember, I have been horribly terrified of horror films. My earliest memory of fear is when I used to have my father come into my room before bedtime, and cast a "magic spell" that would keep my room safe from monsters.*

There are actually products you can buy that have eased the fears of many children. Many have found Native American dream catchers helpful. These are woven circular hangings which, according to legend, catch the bad dreams before they reach the child. Many children feel secure with a dream catcher nearby and report that it does keep the bad dreams away. From time to time I have seen products on the market that advertise themselves as monster blockers or ghost resistors. Children or their parents simply spray these liquids in the closet or the corners of the room, wherever the bad guys are expected to be hiding. Many parents and children report that this type of approach does keep the demons at bay.

The principle here is that the child has to believe that the method or the ritual will keep him safe, and the parent usually has to be willing to go along with the premise. This whole approach may sound bizarre to rational parents who believe that buying into the ritual validates the fear and implies that the demon is real. But you can go along with this ritual without explicitly endorsing the reality status of the evil being. The fear is real—and it's the fear that you're dealing with. You can say, "I know there are no witches, but we can check the closet anyway if it makes you feel better."

An Ounce of Prevention

The methods I've described in this chapter are those that preschool children say they prefer and that have been shown to be effective for many children. Obviously, though, it is difficult to know which one will work best for a particular child and a particular program. Some children's fright may be so intense that these first-line techniques will not be sufficient. Sometimes, for example, the child's experience is truly traumatic or the scary aspect of a particular program comes just at the time a child is dealing with a related, troubling real-life issue. If your child's reaction does not abate over time and truly interferes with

his or her day-to-day activities, don't be afraid to contact
your family physician or a counselor, who can help your
child deal with the problem in more depth.

Remember, too, that some of these fears will take a
while to subside, but most will become manageable over
time. It's good also to remember that many children hide
their fright from their parents because they want to appear more grown-up or they're afraid they might suffer
future restrictions. What is important is your warm and
caring response. What I've noticed in the retrospective reports is that the children who have suffered the most or
who have suffered the longest are those who didn't con-
fide in their parents or whose parents derided their fears
or didn't take them seriously.

Finally, it is very clear that efforts at prevention are well
worth the hassle when weighed against the difficulty of reassuring a young child who has been frightened by something on TV or in a movie. As I've said throughout this
book, many of these responses are remarkably intense, and
they can be very hard to undo. If you happen to be there
when your young child is viewing something potentially
frightening, you can watch for signs of fear. Believe it or
not, a child won't always say, "Mommy, I'm scared!"—but
you may get a grateful nod if you ask whether you should
turn the TV off now. If you're certain a show is frightening,
trust your judgment and turn it off. Even if the child does
not appear scared or admit to being frightened at the time,
things might look different in the middle of the night . . .

CHAPTER EIGHT

Making Explanations Child-Friendly

Reasoning That Comforts Kids

S ome of the coping strategies that help preschoolers can work for older children, too, especially gradual exposure to mild versions of whatever is frightening. But as children get older, they often find that other strategies that worked when they were younger become less effective. They derive less comfort from their favorite stuffed animal, and they become more skeptical about adopting new magical rituals. Also, because older children develop the capacity to process larger amounts of information, it becomes more difficult to distract them from whatever has frightened them. The good news is that with older children you have the option of using verbal strategies. By late elementary school, kids seem to prefer techniques involving words and logical reasoning.

> *I remember having long talks with my mom when I was probably around eight years old, asking her every possible question with the need to know an exact answer in order to be happy. After watching the movie* Halloween *with my family, I was astonished to see that the bad guy, Michael Myers, had disappeared. I needed my mom to assure me that he was not coming back to life to hurt anyone else, more specifically—me. I did not go to bed until all my questions were answered in a way that assured me I would be fine. My mom would tell me that it was impossible that he could come and get me, and that it was just a movie.*

When it comes to scary fantasy shows, older children do well when told to focus on the unreality of the situation. As we saw in the previous chapter, the tell-yourself-it's-not-real strategy is a favorite of older elementary-school children. In the *Wizard of Oz* study, nine- to eleven-year-olds who were told to remember that the witch was not real showed less fear while watching her in a scene, but the same technique did not help preschoolers, who were not fully fluent in the fantasy-reality distinction. Similarly, other researchers have reported that seven- to nine-year-olds had their vampire-movie fears reduced by an explanation of how makeup made the vampires look scary, while five- to six-year-olds were not helped.

Making Verbal Strategies More Effective for Younger Children

Although verbal explanations by themselves tend to be ineffective for preschoolers, there are ways of enhancing their effectiveness. First of all, remember that for preschoolers, seeing is believing. Anything you can do to *show* them something reassuring rather than telling them about it will increase the chances that your strategy will work. For example, in a study involving *The Incredible Hulk,* my colleagues and I tried to counteract children's fears by giving them simple explanations of how the Hulk likes to help people while showing them footage of various scenes in which the Hulk rescues people in distress. This illustrated verbal explanation was effective in reducing fear even in preschool children.

At the end of another study, my colleagues and I gave children hands-on experience with the fear-reducing concept we were trying to get across. For that study, in which we used a scene from the sci-fi thriller *The Blob,* we tried to reassure children by describing the special effects that made the blob look real and letting them create their own "blobs" out of gelatin and food coloring. Talking about and *showing* how scary makeup is applied or allowing children to try on and play with ugly masks may also help them appreciate the make-believe nature of some of the visual images that scare them.

The Challenge of Downplaying Scary Things That Can Happen

Dealing with shows that are not fantasies, however, is decidedly more challenging because there are no easy reassurances. Although fiction may also be considered "make-believe" or "not real" in some sense, those phrases have a very different meaning when applied to fiction than when applied to fantasy, as I discussed in chapter 5. When it comes to reassuring older children about threats they encounter in the media, what is critical is whether what they are seeing *could* happen, not whether that specific event actually *did* happen. Because of this, reducing children's fear in response to fiction is very similar to re-assuring them about something that happened in the news or was shown in a documentary.

It is important to keep in mind that the reassuring aspect of fantasy is the fact that the fantastic things we see could never happen to anyone, anywhere. Witches don't exist, and when children understand and truly accept this fact, we can use it to ease their fear. On the other hand, fiction is a form of make-believe that won't necessarily lend itself to the tell-yourself-it's-not-real strategy. Even though we can tell children, for example, that the char-acter played by Macaulay Culkin in *My Girl* wasn't a real person and he didn't actually die from the bee stings he received in the movie, we can't honestly tell them that no child ever died from a bee sting. Making children understand that the child in that movie did not actually die might ease their sadness about his death, but it is not likely to make them less scared of bees.

It is also a good idea to remember that fantasy programs often contain realistic as well as fantastic elements. Although older children can be reassured that the witch and the flying monkeys in *The Wizard of Oz* will not come after them, many of them are just as frightened by the tornado in that movie, which can't be dismissed so easily.

Dealing with children's exposure to realistic threats and dangers, whether they arise in news reports or in fiction, is a difficult task for parents. These threats arise from sources other than exposure to the mass media, and even adults are not immune to them. One strategy for reducing fears about realistic threats is to provide an explanation that makes the danger seem more remote or less likely to occur. But that technique is difficult to apply successfully. We attempted to do this in the snake study reported in chapter 7. Telling children that most snakes are not poisonous had only a slight tendency to help second and third graders, and the technique backfired completely for children in kindergarten and first grade, making them think more about the poison in snakes than they would have without the explanation.

In the study involving *The Blob* that I referred to earlier in this chapter, we explained to a group of five- to eight-year-olds that a frightening event in a movie could *never* happen anywhere. We told others that the event was very *unlikely* to occur in the area where they lived, hoping that what was unlikely to occur would also seem non-threatening. We told a third group that the event was *highly likely* to occur where they lived. We found, unfortunately, that the children didn't differentiate very well between things that were likely and unlikely to occur. Any possibility that the scary outcome would happen made it equally scary. The only thing that reduced their fear was telling them that it was absolutely impossible.

This finding is consistent with research my colleagues and I have done on children's understanding of concepts related to probability and likelihood. For example, although children in first grade had already grasped the meaning of *definitely*, as in "this will definitely not happen," even many third graders did not understand the difference between an event that would *probably* occur and one that could *possibly* occur. So it's not that reassuring to tell an elementary-school child that the frightening thing they just witnessed is a rare event.

Children older than third grade should become more adept at using information about the small chance of bad things happening. However, research indicates that older children and even adults also overestimate the likelihood of outcomes that are intensely threatening, even when the chances of their happening are infinitesimal. If the possible outcome is catastrophic enough, the thought of any likelihood at all of the event is unacceptable. For this reason, focusing on a frightening event's low likelihood seems to be one of the least effective strategies for reducing the fears of children of any age.

The Calm, Unequivocal, Limited Truth

If minimizing the threat is not helpful, what option do you have? Saying that something that is real is totally impossible is not a good idea because your white lie may come back to haunt you when your child learns the truth elsewhere. If you lose your credibility in this area, your child may stop turning to you for reassurance and lose one of her most powerful resources for coping with fear. On the other hand, if you are not careful, the truth may be interpreted as scarier than it really is. My advice is, Don't lie when talking about realistic dangers, but don't tell your child any more than necessary about the truth. And be sure to phrase your explanation in as calming and unemotional terms as possible.

Returning to the example from the movie *My Girl,* in which a character dies after being attacked by bees, telling your child that very few people die from bee stings is not likely to be very helpful. It would be more effective to say something definite and positive like the following (unless you know it to be false): "You are not allergic to bees, so this can't happen to you."

Let me give you another example of what I mean by saying something definite, reassuring, and positive, using something that happened in my own home. A few years ago, when looking for another program, my son and I accidentally stumbled across a documentary on tornado safety. Unfortunately, as has become increasingly typical, the show was more about the dangers of tornadoes than about how to protect yourself from harm, and it included one especially frightening series of footage taken with a home video recorder during a tornado. The camera was aimed out the window of the house, while several people were heard screaming, "It's here!" "Get down!" and "Where is everybody?" Along with these screams, the camera showed the window being shattered by the high winds. I tried to change the channel, but my son was intent on seeing the program to the end. We watched it together and discussed it afterward.

The first thing Alex asked after the program was over was "Do we have tornadoes in Madison?" Based on my earlier research finding that a local danger will be scary, even if it's very unlikely, I immediately replied, "No," not remembering any that had actually touched down in the city (and, frankly, not wanting to). But my husband corrected me, reminding me of the one that had torn the roof off a car dealership a few years earlier. My next response was to say, truthfully (as far as I know), that we'd never had any tornadoes in Monona, the small suburb of Madison where we actually live. This information was extremely reassuring to Alex, and he went happily off to bed shortly thereafter. I'm sure that that explanation is what made him feel better because for a week or two after that incident, he woke up every morning saying, "I'm so glad we live in Monona." Although I did not say we could never have a tornado here, the fact that I could be so absolute about the past was very reassuring.

The story does not end here, however. As you might imagine, things got more complicated the next time we heard the tornado sirens. As I talked about going down to the basement, Alex said, "But *we* don't have to go down there since we don't have tornadoes here." Thinking quickly, I replied that although we had never had a tornado, we did sometimes get strong, damaging winds, and that it was important to protect ourselves from them as well. This explanation was enough to get him to follow me into the basement without causing him too much anxiety. "Strong damaging winds" got the point across without producing the intense emotional reaction that the idea of a tornado in our town would have produced.

The basic idea, as I see it, in reassuring children about real threats is to provide a truthful explanation that avoids emotional words and that communicates just as much as a child needs to know, but no more. Be ready to answer further questions, but don't go into more details than your child is interested in.

The problem of horrible, real threats that have a small chance of happening seems most acute when dealing with highly publicized cases of child molestation and murder, which are sensationalized on television with increasing

frequency. It's bad enough that we as parents are confronted with these awful possibilities, but we also have to
deal with the fears these stories produce in our children.
When your child asks you how Megan Kanka or Polly Klaas
(or the next highly publicized child victim) was killed,
what's the best thing to say? My advice is to be truthful, yet
as inexplicit as you can be. You can say, for example, that
the child in question was killed by a very sick man, but
spare them any of the details that they do not already
know. The concept of child victimization is frightening
enough that the real details—especially the part about molestation—will only make things immeasurably worse.

What If the Threat Can't Be Minimized?

If you're not successful in convincing your child that what
she's concerned about won't happen, the best approach is
to provide her with the information and tools that will
help her prevent it from happening or at least that will
make her feel more in control of the situation or its outcome. In the study I reported in chapter 1, in which we
showed the schoolhouse burn down in *Little House on the
Prarie,* we ended the session by giving children basic fire-
safety guidelines that they could use in their own lives.
These guidelines were taught with illustrations involving
popular cartoon characters. Children were told, for example, to make sure their home had smoke alarms and to
check to see that the batteries were fresh. They were also
encouraged to have a family escape plan and to practice

family fire drills. Activities such as these, carried out in the home, should be helpful in calming your child's fears of fire if they have already been aroused by a TV show or movie.

For other threats, similar simple protective strategies might be developed. If the fear is of natural disasters, you could review your plans for tornado safety, for example. If the offending movie is about burglars entering the home, you might do a tour of the home, showing how all the doors and windows are securely locked and how the particular technique that the burglar in the TV program used wouldn't work at your house. (Be sure you know this to be true in advance, or avoid the issue.) If the fear is of kidnapping, use the film as an excuse to go over your rules for dealing with strangers. It will help if the child is given an active role in the safety lessons. Going through the motions and role-playing not only the actions but the feeling of being in control of the problem should help.

During my younger years (age eight) I was frightened by daily news reports regarding a kidnapper with a white van that was stalking kids in my town. My parents would sit me down and explain to me that I was smart and that I knew not to talk to strangers and that I knew that if I saw a white van, that I should run away. These talks helped me to cope with the problem because I knew that I wouldn't be taken by surprise—I knew what to do to protect myself.

Sometimes when we try to teach self-protective behaviors to children who are unaware of specific threats, we end up scaring them more than we teach them. But when the mass media thrust these frightening possibilities on our children, we can often turn this unfortunate incident into what educators call a "teachable moment," and make the best of a bad situation.

Of course, not all accidents and disasters are preventable even with protective action, and the older your children become, the better they will understand this. How do you reassure children that nothing like the Oklahoma City bombing will ever happen again? Or that there will never be another midair explosion like the one that downed TWA 800? Or that they could protect themselves in either of these situations? You really can't provide them guarantees, but as they get older, you can stress the protections that have come out of these disasters. We now have better security at federal buildings and in airports, and planes are being redesigned to eliminate the specific causes of well-known crashes. These explanations can only go so far, of course, but your reassurances that we are learning from past mistakes may provide some help.

If All Else Fails, Just Be There and Listen

Simply talking to older children about their fears can also have a tremendously therapeutic effect. Whether the specific content of the discussion helps or not, it seems clear that parental attention, or the calming supportive pres-

ence of another thoughtful human being, is helpful.
Make sure your child knows you are there to listen to her
fright stories, even if you wish she had not seen the program that scared her.

> *The experience of actually watching a scary movie*
> *was not that uncomfortable for me. It was only when I*
> *thought about the films later in the day or before going to*
> *bed that I became frightened. After spending some time*
> *thinking about the scary images and themes of the films,*
> *I would be unable to sleep. Typically, I went back down-*
> *stairs and found my father watching television. He and*
> *I discussed what had scared me and I felt much better.*

As children get older and realize that there are no
guarantees of safety, the act of talking fears over with
someone who takes them seriously may be more beneficial than the actual content of the conversation. I remember a very intense emotional reaction I once had and how
the right kind of sympathetic ear was the only thing that
helped. I was already an adult and my exposure to what
frightened me was probably inevitable, although the tim-
ing could not have been worse. As I was entering my se-
nior year in college, there was a terrible national news
story about eight student nurses who were murdered by a
man named Richard Speck. This man somehow managed
to get himself invited into the students' apartment, where
he brutally killed each of them, one by one. I think one of

them survived, actually, and lived to provide the world with the horrible details. The thought that eight women were no match for one killer was terrifying to me, but the story really hit home not only because I was moving into my first apartment (after three years in the security of the dorms) but because of the similarity of my new apartment to the one the nurses had lived in—both were garden apartments with ground-floor entrances at the front and the back.

The thought of what had happened to these nurses made me feel so vulnerable in my new apartment that I literally could not sleep for what seemed like a week or more. Any sound that I heard in the night, including that of my roommate rolling over in her bed, made me jump or cry out. My reaction was way out of proportion, and I simply couldn't calm myself down. But I had been looking forward to living in an apartment for a long time, and I was embarrassed to tell people about my newfound anxiety.

Fortunately, I soon talked about my problem to a friend who was very sympathetic. He said that if this news story was causing me so much anxiety, I should talk to a therapist about it. In those days, going to a therapist was not as common as it is today, but I thought I'd be willing to do almost anything if it would relieve me of my anxiety.

The interesting thing about this conversation is that after I had decided I would go to see a therapist, I started rehearsing in my mind what I would say to him and what he might say to me, and I suddenly felt in control of the problem. My anxiety immediately started to wane, and it eased so much that I was able to sleep. In fact, I never did make that appointment with the therapist because I had gotten the benefit of having my fears taken seriously by someone who cared. I had discovered that what I was experiencing might be considered reasonable or at least understandable under the circumstances and that there were professionals who helped people in my situation. This discovery was enough to give me back my sense of control.

Of course, solutions are not always that simple. I was lucky. But I'm also confident that a good therapist would have helped me in that situation if I had needed one to get over this trauma.

It is important that you as a parent be ready and willing to discuss your child's fears, even if you can't give her an absolute guarantee of safety. Tell your child that you understand why she's so frightened, even though you don't believe she's in danger. Tell her about this book (if she's old enough, let her read it), and about how frequently the mass media stir up people's fears to levels that are extremely hard to manage. It might help to identify the reasons why this particular program, movie, or event was so terrifying by discussing either how the events were portrayed or how they relate to her current situation. It might also be helpful to tell her about some of your own media traumas and how you succeeded in getting over them. Misery really loves company, particularly company that has been in the same place but has since moved on.

And finally, there is the option of seeking professional help if the fear remains overpowering and out of control.

Balancing Fear with Vigilance

It is true, of course, that this world can be a dangerous place, and children need to be aware of certain threats so that they can protect themselves. A certain amount of fear is necessary for survival. Children need to avoid drowning, for example, without developing a phobia of the water, and they need to protect themselves from child abuse or kidnapping without becoming socially withdrawn. One of the greatest challenges facing parents and other caregivers today lies in striking a balance between a healthy amount of fear and a level that is damaging, while allowing your child to maintain a positive outlook on life.

Of course, after your child's crisis of media-produced fear is over, if it was caused by a fictional program or movie that might have been avoided, it will be a good time to talk about being more careful about programming that makes your child particularly anxious. If your children are in the habit of seeking out the most sensational news stories or the most thrilling movies, they may benefit from your advice that they moderate or curtail their habit.

CHAPTER NINE

Why Kids Are Drawn
to Scary Entertainment

—And What If They Like It Too Much?

Afew years ago, I saw a comic strip in which teenage kids were talking about the upcoming airing of *Gremlins* on television. They were reminiscing about each vicious and gory incident in the movie, saying things like "and when the creature blows up in the microwave—awesome!" The mother of one of the kids, overhearing the conversation, sighs and thinks to herself, "I wonder whatever happened to *The Sound of Music*." To many parents, it's hard to understand why kids are flocking to so many TV programs and movies that we may find overly violent, disturbing, or downright disgusting.

The fact is, if children didn't like to watch scary programs and movies, many of the effects discussed in this book would not occur. If scary programs were not popular, there wouldn't be so many of them on television, and mysteries and horror movies would not be such a staple of the entertainment industry. Although philosophers have pondered for centuries why frightening images are popular, social scientists have only recently begun to explore this question. Most research on the issue relates to why people watch violence. Although not everything that scares children portrays violence and not all violence is scary, most of the things that produce fright relate to violence or the threat of harm in some way.

Why Is There So Much Media Violence?

Nielsen ratings consistently show that most of the Saturday-morning programs with the highest child viewership are violent. Still, there is some debate about whether children really like to watch violence, or whether violent programs are popular simply because there is very little else available for children to watch. The few experiments that have raised or lowered the violence in a program to gauge the effects on children's enjoyment have produced inconsistent results. Clearly, many things work together to determine whether violence is enjoyed, including how it is portrayed and the type of child who is watching.

There are some important economic reasons why violence is found on TV and in the movies as often as it is. One is that commercial TV programs are produced for the widest possible age range. Violent programs are easily understood even by young children, which allows them to capture a very broad audience. A second reason we have so many violent programs and movies is that it is more profitable to produce shows that can be exported to foreign countries. It is a good deal easier to translate violent programs into different languages, and other cultures understand them more readily than programs that deal with issues that are more subtle or more specific to our society.

Social Reasons for Choosing Scary Entertainment

In addition to economic factors, we often see children watching scary shows for social reasons. Scary movies seem to play a role in some sort of rite of passage for teenagers. Several of the students quoted in chapter 5 had experienced especially intense fright reactions to something they had seen at a slumber party. Obviously, slumber-party video viewing is a recent phenomenon since videos only became available about a generation ago. Perhaps it is the modern incarnation of ghost stories told around the campfire. When young people get together in groups for an overnight experience, they often turn to frightening things.

I'm not sure how to explain this tradition. Perhaps scary themes and movies are chosen for sleepovers simply to spice them up and to create an event that will be memorable and distinctly out of the ordinary. Maybe they are used to promote the bonding that often occurs when people go through a negative emotional experience together. Perhaps sleepovers present a safe way to watch the movies the teenagers wouldn't have the nerve to watch if they had to go home to bed alone. Or, watching scary videos together may be a way for youngsters to prove to themselves and to each other that they are tough, grown-up, and brave. In fact, all of these things may go into making scary movies so typical at slumber parties.

You may recall the story of the young boy who "witnessed" *Friday The Thirteenth, Part 2* because he didn't want his friend to consider him a "wussy." He's not alone; it's quite common for boys to watch scary things at the urging of their friends so that they will be considered brave or macho. One boy actually sat through *Jaws* at the age of six:

> . . . *As a result I would have fantasies and nightmares about the blood spurting out of the fisherman's mouth or the shark's teeth piercing his flesh. However, there was one positive aspect of my fright experience, and that was a sense of accomplishment. Even though I felt a little traumatized over the viewing experience, I also felt that I watched something that other people my age couldn't sit through. I would have to speculate that this is because at such a young age there is a great amount of*

competition over what one young boy can stand and what another young boy can stand. To the victor comes a sense of pride and accomplishment.

Psychological Reasons for Viewing

Beyond these economic and social reasons for the popularity of violent, scary entertainment, violence is popular because there is something about it that many people, including children, are attracted to. After reading hundreds of retrospective accounts and reviewing the available research findings, my judgment is that many people are drawn to things that frighten them—often even if they do suffer afterward. The following sentence, taken from an account of *Poltergeist*-induced nightmares, is typical:

We were scared out of our minds but we couldn't take our eyes off the screen or turn off the VCR.

Indeed, it's not hard to find children who say they like to watch violence, plain and simple. For example, when a researcher asked sixth- to eighth-grade children in Milwaukee the question: "Would you watch a television program if you knew it contained a lot of violence?" 82 percent replied "yes." What are some reasons why children, teens, and adults, for that matter, are drawn to violent, scary images? One reason seems to be what is often referred to as morbid curiosity. Even if we don't find it enjoyable or entertaining, many of us can't help joining the crowd around an accident—or, if we don't have the nerve to take a close look, we probably tune into the news that night to find out what happened. We seem to be innately fascinated with (and concerned about) the concept of death, and this seems to draw our attention to violence, death, and injury. If we take an evolutionary perspective here, it stands to reason that animals who paid attention when violence, injury, disease, and death were happening had a better chance of surviving.

Morbid curiosity leads us to want to see certain things that are associated with death. A few years back, for example, it was reported that the charred remains of the Branch Davidian compound outside Waco, Texas, where so many died in a fiery confrontation with the FBI, became such a popular tourist attraction that local officials had to put up a fence. More recently, the house where JonBenet Ramsey was found murdered has also attracted large numbers of the curious. The USA Network reports that whenever it devotes a week to shark programming, its ratings double. Morbid curiosity seems to account, in part, for the success of the "if it bleeds, it leads" philosophy of many news programs, which I talked about in chapter 6. There is something about violent injury and death that draws us in. As one student wrote:

Many people have a curiosity about what it would be like to be in a violent situation, but never allow it to

happen for fear of personal injury. One way to fulfill this
curiosity is to view a violent scene. There is no chance for
personal injury and one can still get a taste of what the
violent situation is like.

Although part of the reason violent portrayals are attractive is that they deal with the frightening notion of death, another part of their attraction for children seems to come from the fact that they are often full of action. Some researchers have even argued that it is action (characters moving fast) rather than violence (characters injuring each other) that attracts children's attention to violent television programs. Clearly both elements are important. Morbid curiosity by itself might lead us to be as fascinated by movies about elderly people passing away quietly or disease victims in the final stages of their illness as we are by shoot-'em-ups, dinosaur attacks, or hand-to-hand combat. But it's clear that there is a much bigger audience for action-packed mayhem than for quieter ways of dying.

One reason for the preference for action-packed violence seems to be that it is arousing. Many people, and children especially, enjoy violent, scary shows because they like the thrill of being stimulated and aroused by entertainment. Viewing violence or watching nonviolent but threatening images temporarily makes children's hearts beat faster and their blood pressure go up. Like adults, many children seek out the feelings produced by violence and suspense to stimulate them when they are bored and take them out of the humdrum of their daily lives. As one veteran of *The Incredible Hulk* put it:

> *This television program scared me to death every time I watched it, yet I tuned in with my mother and younger brother (who was also frightened) each week. I think that there may have been a part of me that enjoyed having my senses aroused. The sound of the high note and the doctor's green eyes got my heart pumping and got me out of the relaxed state in which I usually watch television.*

If there's one characteristic of children that is strongly related to whether or not they're interested in viewing violence, it's their gender. There are many, many studies that show that boys choose to watch violence more often than girls and that they generally enjoy it more. Some psychologists believe that this difference is due to the fact that we treat our little boys differently from our little girls, teaching them that violence is a male, not a female, activity. Other psychologists maintain that boys' greater interest in violence is rooted in their hormones, and that biology predisposes them to be more aggressive and to be more interested in aggressive things. Both factors probably contribute to the fact that boys are more interested than girls in violent toys, violent stories, and violent programs and movies.

It has also been shown that children who are more violent themselves are more interested in viewing violent programs. It's sometimes difficult to know which came first: whether the children became more violent because they watched so much violent programming, or whether their own violent tendencies led them to seek out violent stories to understand or justify their own behavior. The consensus of researchers is that both processes occur. Viewing violence contributes to children becoming more violent, and children who are violent are more interested in viewing violence.

Another reason many children watch violent and scary programs is that they imagine themselves in the place of the characters, and many of them enjoy the feeling of power they get when the good guy, or the character they root for, overcomes dangers and triumphs over the bad guy. One student described his enjoyment of *The Wizard of Oz* this way:

> *I waited with anticipation for each terrifying moment, and from a very early age I enjoyed the emotional buildup and release that came with each one. For me, the resolution that gave the most pleasure was when Dorothy finally killed the Wicked Witch of the West. I was far less concerned with how she got back to Kansas.*

This anecdote leads into another reason for children's attraction to violence, one that deals with fright more directly. Some research shows that watching television crime shows in which the bad guys are punished in the end actually reduces the fears of mildly anxious people. In one study, college students took a six-weeks' heavy dose of action-adventure programs featuring good triumphing over evil. This treatment not only reduced their feelings of anxiety, it increased their appetite for this type of material even after the study was over. Surveys my colleagues and I have done also suggest that some children may choose to watch mildly scary television programs to help them cope with their anxieties. In one survey of parents, for example, we found that children who had been frightened by television were especially interested in violent programs in which good triumphed over evil, but they were not particularly interested in other types of violent programming.

A few programs aimed at children seem to be especially designed to serve the function of reassuring them about their fears. The most obvious one, one that has been on television in various forms since the late sixties, began as *Scooby-Doo, Where Are You?* This animated program features a group of teenage kids and a dog or two who travel around in their van and solve mysteries involving monsters, ghosts, mummies, abominable snowmen, and the like. Scooby, the canine star, and Shaggy, one of the teenagers, are always extremely frightened by the threatening beast or monster. Their fear is dramatized humorously, with chattering teeth, trembling bodies, and cries of "Get me out of here!"

Each plot of *Scooby-Doo* is nearly identical to the others: Someone has concocted a scheme to steal something valuable by scaring everyone else. To accomplish his goal, the villain dons some sort of scary costume and arranges other special effects to convince the general public they had better stay away. In every episode, the kids figure out the mystery and confront the villain, revealing that there is a real person inside the monster costume. The kids are then praised for their heroism and their ability to solve the mystery, and they explain the very complicated set of clues that helped them discover who the villain really was. The obvious message is, Things aren't as scary as they seem, and you, too, can overcome your fear.

Although most kids don't even consider this a scary program, it seems that some children who are confronting fears turn to programs like this to work through their anxieties. The program produces a very safe level of fear that the young child can easily master and shows that other people (and even a dog!) have anxieties that they can learn to control. Other mildly scary programs that show a hero in danger but ultimately triumphing over it seem to have a similar effect.

But there's a definite limit to the effectiveness of television and movies as an anxiety reducer. I talked in chapter 7 about a fear-reducing technique called desensitization, which exposes a child to something that's feared in weak, manageable doses. It is important to note that an effective fear-reducing strategy must provide only a very mild dose of fear, one that the child can easily learn to handle. Something intensely frightening will more than likely have the opposite effect, making the child's fears even stronger and more difficult to allay.

The Anxious, Traumatized Child vs. the Jaded Kid Who Can't Get Enough

Although mildly anxious children may turn to safe levels of violence to reassure themselves, children experiencing intense anxieties generally don't enjoy watching violent television. In a study of children in inner-city Milwaukee, children who were experiencing acute anxiety symptoms from the real violence in their environment were the least interested in viewing very violent shows and were the most upset when they did watch them. Rather than helping these children cope, viewing violence made them feel worse.

But there were other children in the Milwaukee study who reacted quite differently to their violent surroundings. These children seemed to have become emotionally numb to real violence, showing very little trauma and few anxiety symptoms. It was these children who were especially interested in viewing very violent programs. Not only were these children more interested in viewing violence; they said they felt especially good when watching people on violent shows fight and hurt each other. Even more disturbing, the more interested these kids were in viewing violence on TV, the less they cared to see the bad guys get caught. These tough kids who had seen it all seemed to like violence for violence's sake. They liked the thrill of the fight and couldn't care less if the good guy won in the end.

Although children who are callous and numb may be less likely to have nightmares and other fear reactions, what is worrisome about this group is that they are more prone to other effects of witnessing violence and especially prone to the negative effects of desensitization.

The Downside of Desensitization

When I talked about desensitization as a coping strategy in chapter 7, it was in a positive context. But desensitization can be taken to an extreme when the child is exposed to large amounts of violence and other threatening images. As a result of repeated exposure to intense violence, children and adults show a lessening of their emotional response to it. They are then likely to seek out more intense levels of violence to achieve the same thrill that lower levels used to give them.

Research shows that children who watch a lot of violence become less aroused by it over time and that children become less bothered by real interpersonal aggression after watching fictionalized violence. Research also shows that repeated exposure to violence leads to less sympathy for its victims and to the adoption of violent attitudes and behaviors.

The trend for children and teenagers to become desensitized to violence is especially disturbing if we take a look at movies that are being made today. I remember how intense reactions were to such groundbreaking movies as *Bonnie and Clyde* and *The Wild Bunch* in the sixties. But in retrospect, these movies are very mild compared to popular movies of today like *Natural Born Killers*. What is worse, now that there are so many television channels, and almost all movies are available on video, teenagers who enjoy super-violent programming have a virtually unlimited supply of intense mayhem. The prevalence and easy availability of emotion-deadening viciousness makes the desensitization of large numbers of children a higher risk now than ever before.

In sum, then, there are a variety of reasons why your child may want to view violent, scary programs: Some of these are social, relating to the desire to demonstrate "manliness" or to engage in an adolescent rite of passage, some are psychological, and some may actually benefit your child—if he chooses a manageable dose of a threat that he learns to master. But heavy doses of brutality result in one of two unhealthy outcomes: either the severe fright reactions that this book describes or the deadening of emotional responsiveness and antisocial attitudes toward violence.

The fact that children may be attracted to scary programs certainly complicates the task of parents who want to shield their children from unnecessary trauma. The next chapter deals with the issue of ratings, program and movie labels that are intended to help parents make more informed decisions about what their children should watch. As we will see, not only are ratings sometimes misleading, they often make parents' jobs harder by making hazardous programs and movies more appealing.

CHAPTER TEN

Ratings Roulette

. . . .

The Perils of "Parental Guidance"

A mother recently told me the following story:

> *We told our son that he would be getting a new ten-speed bike for his thirteenth birthday. But he told us he wouldn't need a new bike. He declared that he wouldn't have time to ride it after he was thirteen, since he would be spending all his free time watching PG-13 movies!*

Having read this far, I hope you're convinced of two things: First, it is extremely important to be aware of and to guide what your child sees on television, in videos, and at the movies. And second, it may be more difficult than you thought to shield your child from programs you consider inappropriate. Although you may think that your home, at least, is your castle, that castle has no moat and no fortress to protect it from the televised intruders that may disturb your children. Some of the intruders may seem harmless on the surface, but they conceal a seamier side. And to make things even more difficult, your children may be curious about these very intruders and may be eager to invite them in, despite your concerns.

I want to talk now about some practical problems of managing television in your home and selecting movies or videos for your children. Once you've decided that you want to be selective in what your children watch, how can you know in advance what will be in a program, video, or movie?

One way, of course, would be to watch every program or movie before your child sees it. Although this would perhaps be an ideal solution, no parent has the time to do it, and it's simply not feasible when we're talking about watching live television. So we have to depend on various forms of information that are provided to us. We have had movie ratings since the sixties, and now we have television ratings as well. Let's look at each of these in turn.

What You Should Know about Movie Ratings

When choosing a movie or a video for your child, the most obvious bit of information you have to go on besides its title is its Motion Picture Association of America (MPAA) rating. Most parents are familiar with this system, which puts movies into four major categories: G for "General

Audiences," PG for "Parental Guidance Suggested," PG-13 for "Parents Strongly Cautioned," and R for "Restricted." A fifth rating, NC-17, "No One 17 and Under Admitted," was recently added, but it is rarely used.

The MPAA employs a committee of parents, who screen the movies and give them ratings by majority vote. A movie producer who is unhappy with a rating can re-edit the film and resubmit it or submit the film to an appeals board, headed by MPAA president Jack Valenti, who developed the system in the 1960s.

Many parents take note of a movie's MPAA rating in making selections for their children, but these ratings have been widely criticized for being much too vague and too arbitrary. The rating system gives rough age guidelines regarding who should be allowed to see the movie, but it does not say why a movie received its rating. A PG rating, for example, indicates that many parents may consider some material unsuitable for their children, but it doesn't give any clue as to what's in the movie that makes it unsuitable.

Although the MPAA ratings do not indicate why a program received the rating it did, this information is available in other locations. Bowing to public pressure, the MPAA has provided content information for all movies that have received a rating of PG or higher since 1995. This information is usually not available in movie advertisements or on videocassette labels. However, it is often included in movie reviews, and it can be accessed through the MPAA's web site (www.mpaa.org), by subscription to the *Motion Picture Rating Directory* (at a cost of $160 per year), and by telephone in some cities.

As a researcher interested in this issue, and as a mother who finds it difficult to locate suitable movies for my own child to view, I thought it would be interesting to use the *Motion Picture Rating Directory* to determine the proportion of movies that were given the various ratings. What I found may surprise you, but it does explain why it's so hard to find movies that are obviously intended for young children. Out of some fourteen hundred movies that the MPAA rated in 1995 and 1996, only 3 percent were rated G. During that time, 14 percent were rated PG, 16 percent were rated PG-13, and a whopping 67 percent were rated R!

Because the G rating is so rare, many parents look to movies rated PG as the next best option. But without the additional content information, they are left in the dark in terms of what to expect. I became curious to know how many PG-rated movies simply had bad language, for example. I had heard members of the movie industry admit that very few producers actually want a G rating because they're afraid that only very young children will want to see their movie. (And as we'll see later in this chapter, their fears are well grounded!) Adding a few bad words is one way to avoid a G rating, and, looking at the reasons the MPAA gave for all the movies that were rated PG in 1995 and 1996, my colleagues and I found that more than one-fourth of them (26 percent) had bad language only. Many parents feel that these bad words are the lesser of the three evils that are prevalent in movies (language, sex, and violence). If only the rating would tell parents which were the ones with language!

And how helpful is the PG rating in letting us know what to expect in terms of other types of content? In addition to those with bad words, 12 percent of PG movies had violence only and another 26 percent had both violence and bad language. Eighteen percent of PG-rated movies had no violence, no sex, and no bad language. Most of these were described as having "thematic elements" that were somehow inappropriate for young children. So it's quite clear that the PG rating tells parents virtually nothing about the content to expect in a movie. If they can't access the MPAA's web site or find the content reasons in another location, they are left almost completely in the dark.

There's another little-known problem with the PG rating that I came upon in my analyses. When my colleagues and I looked at the content of a random sample of movies shown on television, there was only a whisper of a difference between movies rated PG and those rated PG-13. It was then that I was reminded that the PG-13 rating was not introduced until 1984. This rating was added in response to children's fright reactions to such movies as *Gremlins* and *Indiana Jones and the Temple of Doom*. Before that time, movies that now would be given a PG-13 rating were probably rated PG. Did you know, for example, that *Jaws*—the movie cited so many times as causing long-term fears—is rated only PG? Certainly that movie deserves more of a caution than "Parental Guidance Suggested." But it was released before the PG-13 rating existed. So, in addition to other problems with the MPAA ratings, it's important to find the date of a movie's release when interpreting the PG rating. If a PG-rated movie was released before 1984, its content may bring an especially upsetting surprise.

Can't We Even Trust the G Rating?

The G rating doesn't necessarily help us either. As one mother who answered a recent nationwide survey of ours put it:

> As of now, I do not trust the MPAA's ratings at all. Not even G.

The G rating is not necessarily safe for young children. The label "General Audiences: All Ages Admitted" appears comforting to most parents, although the explanation of the rating supplied by MPAA president Jack Valenti hedges a bit:

> This is a film which contains nothing in theme, language, nudity and sex, violence, etc. which would,

in the view of the Rating Board, be offensive to
parents whose younger children view the film. The
G rating is not a "certificate of approval," nor does
it signify a children's film.

The explanation goes on to say that a G-rated movie has
no nudity or sex and that "the violence is at a minimum."

If there's one type of movie where the G rating especially falls down on the job, it's the animated feature. Although most of these fairy tale or adventure movies are
rated G, many of them have a good deal more than mini-
mal violence. For example, the G-rated *Beauty and the
Beast* is intensely violent, both in the vicious attacks by the
wolves on the Beast, and in the fierce, deadly battle between the Beast and the villain Gaston. In a story in the
Boston Globe, one mother complained that the wolves in
this movie had caused her three-year-old daughter to become terrified of dogs, and that her daughter was still
afraid of dogs three years later.

Although it may seem shocking to those who have always believed cartoon features to be designed for young
children, my own research and the frequency of parents'
reports of their children's distress lead me to conclude
that many of them are too scary for many children below
the age of six. Some parents who agree with me on this
have confided that many of their friends think they're
crazy. If animated features can't be rated G, what use is
there in the G rating at all?

This last question brings up a very good point. Animated fairy tale and adventure films seem to be rated on the basis of their target market—children—rather than the effects they have on children. A G rating is not an indication of content. And it is not very helpful to parents.

Just Let Us Know What's in the Show

To summarize some of the problems with movie ratings: We can't tell what's in the movie from the rating alone; we can't interpret PG ratings that were issued before 1984 (when PG-13 was introduced); and we can't trust the G rating to be safe for preschoolers. MPAA ratings reflect what a committee of parents think would be offensive to other parents. They do not reflect any expertise in the field of child psychology or knowledge of the impact of the media on children. These ratings are not helpful in predicting the effects a movie will have on your child.

What *would* help us make viewing decisions for our children? The answer is, an honest indication of what is in the movie. If a rating simply indicated the movie's contents, parents could ask themselves, "Is my child ready to watch this?"

Take another striking example of a G-rated animated feature, *Bambi*. In the middle of this classic movie, the sweet young fawn's mother is shot and killed by a hunter. When I went to a matinee where *Bambi* was playing, I heard interesting conversations all around me. After the hunter's shot rang out, and while Bambi was searching in vain for his mother, I heard many children asking the same question: "What happened to Bambi's mother?" I also noticed that different parents were answering in different ways—some were being honest, but others didn't want to communicate the brutality of the truthful answer. If you take your preschooler to *Bambi,* be prepared for your child to suddenly confront the thought of *you* dying. I often hear reports of preschoolers' problems with *Bambi,* yet it's hard to get the message out that it's better to wait with this movie. What could sound more innocent than a G-rated cartoon named *Bambi?* Wouldn't information about what happens in this movie serve you better than the rating?

There are scary scenes in many animated fairy tale and adventure features. In addition to the recurrent theme of the loss of the mother, there are a multitude of monstrous and grotesque villains. There are also many disturbing character transformations, and there's plenty of intense violence. This is the stuff of nightmares for two- to five-year-olds. These films are often fun for slightly older children, perhaps six or seven and up, but they can be too much for younger ones to take. My advice is not to take the safety of any so-called children's movie for granted, but to err on the side of caution if you have any doubts.

I want it to be clear that this recommendation is not an attack on the entertainment industry; nor is it intended to single out any specific producers of children's movies. This is information for parents who are seeking enjoyment—not nightmares—for their children. All children are not equally sensitive to this type of material, but enough of them respond badly that discretion is warranted.

Members of the movie industry may be alarmed at the advice I'm giving because they may see it as potentially cutting into the audience for their G-rated movies. But I am not advising you to boycott these movies; simply wait until your child is old enough to see them without trauma. Who knows, if a child's first experience with the movies is a fun thrill rather than a series of sleepless nights, maybe that child will become a more avid consumer of movies in the long run!

Making the Most of Movie Ratings

In spite of all the problems with movie ratings, they do provide *some* information. Most R-rated movies and a high proportion of those rated PG-13 have enough sex, violence, and bad language to eliminate them as an option for young children. And you can use the MPAA's web site to get some idea of the reasons why recent movies received their ratings. To me, the best use of the MPAA ratings is to rule out movies with more restrictive ratings (unless you have viewed them yourself, and know the rating to be wrongly applied). And don't be reassured by the lower-level ratings of G or PG without getting further information about the content of the movie. (A video guide might be a good place to start.) A table in the appendix summarizes important features of the movie ratings.

What About TV Ratings?

Although there are many difficulties in selecting movies and videos for your children, the stakes are even higher for television because TV programs come into your home automatically. For all the channels your set receives, the programs are there at the touch of a remote. Unless some program-blocking technology is in place, or you are monitoring your TV at all times, their availability in your home is out of your control.

Fortunately, we are entering a new era, one in which parents are being given new tools to help them screen out certain types of programs. The Telecommunications Act of 1996 required new television sets to be manufactured with an electronic device known as a V-chip within a specified period of time. The V-chip reads a code or rating that is embedded in each program as it is transmitted. Parents decide which rating levels are inappropriate for their child, and by flipping a switch, they ensure that no programs with those ratings will be shown on their TV unless they themselves choose to override the blocking.

The concept seems simple enough, but the complicating and controversial part is how programs are rated. Someone has to give each program a rating that parents will find useful in deciding whether or not a program should be blocked.

The Tug-of-War over the TV Ratings: Parents vs. the Television Industry

In February of 1996, shortly after the Telecommunications Act was passed, the leaders of the broadcast, cable, and film industries agreed to come up with a rating system to apply to their programs. Many of these leaders were reluctant to provide ratings because of their fears that the ratings might lower viewership for their programs and ultimately reduce their profits. But with the threat that someone else might create a system if they did not, they set up the Ratings Implementation Group headed by MPAA president Jack Valenti. Because of the volume of programs that would need to be rated, it was assumed from the start that producers or distributors would rate their own programs rather than having a committee determine the ratings. Unfortunately, under Valenti's leadership, it was also assumed that the TV ratings would be based on the movie ratings that he developed.

Although Valenti's group publicly acknowledged that ratings were for parents, many people, myself included, were concerned that economic forces in the industry would outweigh parents' wishes in determining the type of rating system that would emerge. So, in the summer of 1996, I joined with the National PTA and the Institute for Mental Health Initiatives (IMHI) to do a nationwide survey to find out what parents wanted in a rating system. We explored whether parents preferred the MPAA approach, which gives age guidelines but doesn't specify content, or a content-based approach, which indicates the level of sex, violence, and coarse language in a program, but gives no age recommendations. This second approach is similar to a system that has been used for years on the cable channels HBO, Showtime, and Cinemax.

We sent our survey to a random sample of the PTA's national membership, and the results came back from every state in the country. These parents voted overwhelmingly for information about content: 80 percent of them chose a content-based system, while only 20 percent felt the system should give age recommendations. Our findings were echoed in two other national polls in the fall of 1996 and in several others after that.

Although the entertainment industry engaged in a very public process of consulting with researchers and child advocates while developing their rating system, they ignored our unanimous recommendations for a content-based system and came out with the TV Parental Guidelines in December of 1996, based primarily on the MPAA ratings. Instead of G, PG, PG-13, and R, the new ratings were TV-G, "General Audience"; TV-PG, "Parental Guidance Suggested"; TV-14, "Parents Strongly Cautioned"; and TV-MA, "Mature Audience Only." The new rating system also had two other levels, to be used for what the industry dubbed "children's programming": TV-Y for "All Children" and TV-Y7, "Directed to Older Children." The rating system, which is designed to be applied to all programs with the exception of news and sports, was adopted by all channels except PBS (the Public Broadcasting System) and BET (Black Entertainment Television). PBS said the ratings as designed were uninformative; BET objected to the concept of ratings per se.

Problems with the Industry's Rating System

As if the fact that American parents overwhelmingly preferred a system of content indicators rather than age guidelines wasn't sufficient evidence to force the TV industry to change its mind, there were other problems with the TV Parental Guidelines as well.

The TV rating system provided no information at all about why a program got its rating. At least with the MPAA ratings, parents now have the web site available to find out about content and we have the assurance that a committee of our peers has determined the rating a movie received. But with the TV Parental Guidelines, not only were no parents involved in determining a program's rating, none were involved in the appeals process either. In fact, no one outside the industry was permitted to sit on the Monitoring Board for the new rating system. So much for serving parents!

But the report card was even worse for the TV Parental Guidelines: Guess how this type of rating affects children!

"The cooler the movie, the higher the rating."

This spontaneous comment came from a ten-year-old girl who participated in research my colleagues and I conducted for the National Television Violence Study, an independent violence monitoring project funded by the cable TV industry. The aim of the research was to determine whether putting warning labels or restrictive ratings on violent shows would discourage children from viewing them, or whether the attempt would backfire and make children more interested in seeing them—the forbidden-fruit effect. In the study this girl participated in, which involved children between the ages of five and eleven, a child and his or her parent selected the programs the child would see. Some of the program choices the pair was given had the label "Contains some violence. Parental discretion advised." Other choices involved movies that were rated PG-13: "Parents Strongly Cautioned."

What was most interesting about this study was the difference between how parents and children talked about the programs' labels. Almost all the comments the parents made about the programs with restrictive labels were negative. In contrast, more than half of the children's comments about these programs ranged from favorable to downright enthusiastic. For example, one child said, "PG-

13. Choose that one!" Another blurted out, "Parental discretion advised—that's awesome!" These cautionary labels really added to the programs' allure for many children.

My colleagues and I also did some studies to find out how these ratings affect kids who make viewing decisions in the absence of their parents. We found that boys were more interested in a program when it was labeled "parental discretion advised" than when it came without a label. We also found that children between ten and fourteen were much more interested in a movie when they were told it was rated PG-13 or R and much less interested in the same movie if they thought it was rated G. Among younger children, those who were the most aggressive or who liked to watch TV the most also found programs with restrictive ratings more enticing. On the other hand, content-based systems like the one used by HBO and Showtime did not attract children to programs with higher violence levels.

These studies show that ratings like those the TV industry developed are the most likely to attract our children to the programs we want to shield them from! Telling a child "you're too young for this program" and telling parents "protect your child from this" makes a program much more tantalizing. Simply providing information about the content, the way HBO and Showtime do, is not nearly as provocative.

Unfortunately then, rather than helping you, TV ratings may very well make it harder for you to protect your child from inappropriate programs. Many parents have reported this problem, including a mother who said that her ten-year-old son had suddenly become so fascinated with anything rated TV-14 that it was causing immense conflict in her family. Another mother told me that her fourteen-year-old daughter, who had previously accepted her parents' restriction on *NYPD Blue,* suddenly insisted she was entitled to see it after it began being labeled TV-14. So it seems that age-based ratings can cause problems with children both under and over the recommended age minimum. At least the V-chip may allow parents to block a program without calling their child's attention to the forbidden fruit. But it may be a long time before most TV sets are equipped with blocking technology.

The Compromise Rating System:
The Good, the Bad, and the Complicated

The TV industry's rating system met an unprecedented throng of opponents, who joined together in the spring and summer of 1997 to pressure for changes. The National PTA led a coalition of public health and child advocacy groups, including the American Medical Association, the American Academy of Pediatrics, the American Psychological Association, the Center for Media Education, and the Children's Defense Fund. These groups relentlessly lobbied Congress and the Federal Communications Commission (FCC), asking them to insist on a better system. The television industry countered that all the criticism was coming from these "special interest groups," as they called them, and maintained that most parents were satisfied with the ratings the industry was providing. However, after comments to the FCC and a congressional hearing in Peoria, Illinois, showed how widespread parents' opposition was, the industry started to negotiate with the child advocacy groups, and most channels agreed to a compromise rating system in July of 1997. At that time, PBS agreed to use the new system and BET maintained its refusal to rate its programs. NBC refused to adopt the compromise system and continued to use the age-based ratings.

The compromise system, which began being applied to programs on October 1, 1997, keeps the original age-based system but adds various content indicators to help parents determine what, specifically, caused the program to receive its rating. The upper three ratings (TV-PG, TV-14, and TV-MA) may now be accompanied by a V for violent content, an L for coarse language, an S for sexual content, and a D for sexual dialogue or innuendo. For children's programs, an FV may be added to the TV-Y7 rating to indicate that the program contains "fantasy violence." The amended television rating system is shown in the appendix.

The fact that the industry budged at all—Jack Valenti had warned critics that he'd see them in court "in a nanosecond" if they tried to force any changes—is a great victory for parents. This is one instance where parents' voices were heard, and we should all feel indebted to the child advocacy groups and to members of Congress, particularly Representative Ed Markey of Massachusetts and Senator John McCain of Arizona, who kept the pressure on the television industry. The additional content information will undoubtedly be helpful.

Problems with the Amended System

The bad news is that the compromise rating system keeps some unfortunate features of the original system because the industry adamantly refused to give up on its age-based rating structure. First, the fact that the age guidelines have been retained makes it likely that the forbidden-fruit effect will continue, making restricted programs more tantalizing to many children. Second, the new system does not require full disclosure when some types of content are less controversial than others within the same program. Under the compromise, the overall rating of a program is determined by its most intense content. In other words, if a program has "strong coarse language," it is rated TV-14-L; if it has "moderate violence," it is rated TV-PG-V. But if it has both of these elements, it is still rated TV-14-L, and no mention is made of its violent content. What this means is that if a movie is rated TV-14 or TV-MA, it may have lower levels of sex, violence, or coarse language that are not explicitly indicated by a content letter.

Another problem with the compromise is that the industry insisted on using euphemisms rather than describing content clearly and accurately. Although the parent groups had argued for using a V for violence, an S for sex, and an L for coarse language, the industry insisted upon adding D for situations in which sex is talked about but not shown. They also balked at using the word "violence" to refer to the mayhem that goes on in many children's shows, such as *Power Rangers* or *The X-Men*. Instead, the amended system uses the letters FV to refer to "fantasy violence." Any intense violence that occurs in children's programs is labeled fantasy violence, whether the violence is indeed of the impossible variety or whether it is quite realistic but simply appears in a children's show.

Finally, it remains to be seen whether producers will assign ratings accurately and consistently to their programs.

The compromise system is complicated, but at least it permits parents to receive some information about the type of content in a program and, importantly, the agreement added five representatives of child advocacy groups to the Monitoring Board of the rating system. If television producers assign ratings arbitrarily or irresponsibly, there are some members of the monitoring group who are beholden to families rather than to the television industry's bottom line.

Alternative Rating Systems

There are a number of groups that are dissatisfied with the TV Parental Guidelines and that have developed their own systems for rating television content. One of these groups, the Children's Television Consortium, is especially concerned that the television industry's system is not informed by the findings of medical or psychological research. They have developed a system called Our Kids TV (OKTV), based on what is known about the effects of television on children. This system will be especially helpful to parents who are concerned about their children's fright reactions because it has a separate set of ratings dealing with horror, based heavily on my research about what frightens children at different ages.

One handicap of the OKTV system is that unless the raters are provided with advance information about the content of specific episodes of programs, they may lack the important details necessary to rate them accurately. Another problem involves the public's access to the ratings: Newspapers are unlikely to provide alternative ratings in their program listings. Moreover, the television industry is not likely to embed such ratings in their program transmission, rendering them unreadable by the V-chip. Nevertheless, because these ratings will undoubtedly be much more useful to parents than the industry's system, it may well be worthwhile to take the extra effort to locate them. When the OKTV system is up and running, you will be able to obtain information about it through the web site of the American Academy of Child and Adolescent Psychiatry (www.aacap.org).

This chapter has suggested how movie and television ratings may be of value and has also pointed out some of their deficiencies. Now it's time to see how best to put what you've learned in this book into day-to-day practice. After all, it's up to you to manage your child's TV viewing and make the best of ratings and new technologies. It is also important that you speak up and be sure your opinions and needs are listened to by the larger community.

CHAPTER ELEVEN

Taming the Resident Monster

. . . .

Living with the Reality of Television,
Movies, and Videos

Guiding or Controlling Your Child's Viewing

Now that you've seen some of the effects of frightening media fare on children and know some of the ways to predict what will be especially disturbing for your child, let's look at some of the day-to-day techniques that you can use to reduce the chances of negative effects. What *can* you do as a parent who wants to coexist responsibly with television in your home and who wants to make sensible movie and video choices? There are a number of things that can help you.

Limit the amount of time your child spends watching television, especially around bedtime. Limiting viewing is a good idea for other reasons than reducing your child's exposure to frightening fare. Many studies show that viewing more than one or two hours of television a day interferes with a child's other activities, and the effects can be seen on performance in school as well as in children's social interactions. Recognize that a lot of TV viewing is done out of boredom. To me, one of the most unhealthy aspects of television is that a child can sit in front of the set for long periods of time doing nothing, yet not feeling bored. If the television set suddenly broke down, how long do you think your child would last sitting there on the couch? If some of your child's viewing is prompted by boredom, try getting your child involved in other activities. I realize this is easier said than done, but most kids will stop watching television more willingly if you offer them something else to do rather than simply tell them to stop watching.

Become actively involved in your children's television viewing. This means not only setting up rules for their viewing and guiding their choices of shows but also being aware of what they are watching, sitting down and watching television with them, and having a discussion about what you have seen. By becoming familiar with the different programs your child watches, you can make a more informed judgment about which programs are relatively safe and unlikely to produce fear. In addition, you can be there to monitor the programs you're less sure of. For very young children, you can be ready with the remote to change the channel if the program seems to be veering in a harmful direction. For older children, you can be ready to discuss any troubling issues the program may raise.

There's another benefit to being involved in your child's viewing: Our research on TV ratings and advisories showed that children whose parents watch TV with them and discuss it with them are less likely to choose restricted content when their parents are not around. Those children seem to understand the reasons for their parents' restrictions and are more likely to accept them. As in other areas of child rearing, many children are more likely to accept a restriction if it seems to be arrived at cooperatively and for good reasons, rather than being delivered in an authoritarian fashion. Explaining the reasons for your decisions in a nonjudgmental way is more likely to bring success than simply criticizing the program or your child's taste. You'd do better to say, "We're not going to watch this because it causes nightmares" than to say, "That's garbage—turn it off."

If you can't watch a program or movie in advance or view it with your child, find out as much as you can about the show. Read whatever is available. Many movie reviewers give special attention to things they think might be frightening for young children. I hope that this book will make reviewers more sensitive to some of the specific things that frighten children of different ages, so that reviews will become even more helpful. Talk to the parents of your children's friends as well, checking for any problems their children may have had.

Use whatever information you can get from the rating systems. For movies released in 1995 or later, check the MPAA's web site for content information. For television programs, the amended TV rating system, with all its problems, does give parents advance information that has not been available in the past. In addition to the general age guidelines, there should be an indication (if the rating is done fairly) of the presence of violence, sex, coarse language, and sexual dialogue. This information should permit you to tailor your viewing decisions to your own values and your own concerns about the members of your family. I'll remind you here that much of what frightens children is violent, and there is a great deal of research that shows other harmful effects of viewing violent programs: They can lead to a reduction in empathy for the victims of violence and to the adoption of violent attitudes and behaviors. If you are mainly concerned about your child's exposure to violence, you can be especially wary of children's programs with the FV label and general programming with a V label.

Research also shows that many parents are concerned about their children's exposure to sexual dialogue, sexual situations, and coarse language, and that parents differ in terms of how strongly they worry about the effects of different types of content. If your child's exposure to coarse language concerns you, you can avoid programs with an L; if you feel your child is ready to be exposed to sexual dialogue and innuendo but not to actual depictions of sex, you can avoid programs with an S, but you don't have to worry so much about programs with the designation D. It's up to you.

The V-chip, when available, will allow you to implement your ratings decisions automatically. With a V-chip, you can designate which age-based ratings (for example, TV-14 and up) and content indicators (for example, V or S) are inappropriate for your children, and then all programs with those ratings will be blocked from your set. Only you, or someone else who knows your secret password or code number, will be able to override your decisions. You can think of the V-chip as a sieve over the pipeline that lets television programs into your home. You set the size and shape of the openings to sift out programs whose ratings are unacceptable to you. This gives you an unprecedented form of control over what enters your home through your television. The advantage of the V-chip is that it is mandated, beginning mid-1999, for most new televisions, so it will be much cheaper and more convenient than other devices that are purchased separately.

Look for other blocking technologies beyond the V-chip. The V-chip is not the only way to automatically block programs from entering your home, and it is important to understand the distinction between the V-chip, which is mandated for new television sets, and other blocking technologies that are created on a voluntary basis and will often be sold separately from televisions. Because the V-chip is the result of a governmental mandate, there are limits, politically, to how far it will go. In March of 1998, the FCC approved the technological standard for the V-chip, and few television-set manufacturers are likely to install V-chips that go beyond the FCC's requirements. According to the FCC's mandate, V-chips will be able to read the TV Parental Guidelines and the MPAA ratings, but will not have the capability to read any alternative rating systems that other groups are developing. Moreover, the V-chip will not permit parents the option of blocking unrated programs. Therefore, a family who uses the V-chip will have no protection from news or sports or from any other programs that a channel does not rate.

But what the government *requires* in new TV sets doesn't limit what a manufacturer can produce voluntarily or what a parent can hope to have in other blocking technologies. In terms of technological feasibility, there are many ways blocking devices can go further than the V-chip. Shouldn't you, as an individual parent, have the ability to keep programs out of your home if you're concerned about their effects on your child? One obvious option you should have is the ability to block unrated programs, like the news. The government-mandated V-chip will never block the news because news programs are exempt from ratings. But the news, as we have seen, contains some of the scariest television there is. In early Canadian trials of the V-chip, parents had the option of blocking all unrated programs if they wanted to, and many of them understandably chose that option.

Having read this book, you will also recognize that blocking devices that are based on the TV industry's rating system will be only partially successful in screening out scary material, even in programs that are rated. If TV producers honestly report the contents of their programs, you should be able to block out programs that are explicitly violent by using ratings, but the TV ratings are not sensitive to many of the things that this book has shown are especially scary to preschoolers. Vicious-looking animals, grotesque or deformed characters, and frightening transformations, for example, will not necessarily be captured in the violence codes, so it will be up to you to screen for these scary elements. The OKTV ratings, described at the end of chapter 10, may be helpful in identifying these frightening elements.

Other aspects of television that are left unrated, and that the FCC-mandated V-chip is unable to block, are advertisements and promos for future programs, and as we have seen, promos can be especially frightening for children even though they may be as brief as thirty seconds. Because of this, blocking entire channels may be more useful than blocking by ratings when protecting preschoolers, especially. No matter how many channels your home receives, there are probably only a few that are reasonably safe for young children most of the time. A few channels are sensitive to the needs of young viewers, and they tend not to advertise for scary programs during shows aimed at preschoolers. You might be more at ease, then, if you let in only those channels that you trust when you're not in the room; you can override this blocking when you're there to help with specific selections.

There are several set-top devices available or in development that provide a variety of different program-blocking options. Some simply retrofit a V-chip to older sets to allow you to block on the basis of the TV industry's rating system and the MPAA ratings without having to buy a new TV. But others are likely to provide additional services, and it will be worth the effort to seek out the ones that provide the most effective protection. Look for a device that allows you to block unrated programs in addition to allowing you to block according to rating levels. Not only will this option let you block news and sports, it will turn the entire concept of TV reception upside down. Rather than allowing you only to block programs that have ratings that indicate they might be objectionable, it will put you in the position of inviting into your home only those programs whose ratings are acceptable. With the ability to block unrated programs, you can decide, for example, to let in only programs rated TV-Y. To my mind, this is the way television should be. After all, it is *your* home, and they are *your* children.

Other helpful features to look for are the ability to block entire channels and the ability to block individual programs that you know disturb your own child. Some of these features may be available in newer TV models. Your current set may already have them. If not, shop around for the best blocking features when you buy your set-top box or your next TV.

If all of these features are not currently available, the electronics industry will likely produce them if they sense that there is enough consumer demand. Don't hesitate to let your local electronics dealer know what would help you.

Recognize that you will often have to make different program and movie choices for your different-aged children. I realize that this may be one of the toughest recommendations to swallow, but the sad fact that this book reports is that one child's thrill is often his younger brother or sister's sleepless week. Again and again, the horror stories I hear involve a younger sibling being exposed to something she never would have chosen herself. I've included a summary in the appendix of what children of different ages find disturbing. Be firm with your older children about not subjecting the younger ones to trauma, and try to find a way for them to see what's appropriate for their age when the younger ones are off doing something else. Older kids may need to tape their shows and watch them later in the evening. When renting videos, there may be times when you have to rent two. One for now, and one for after the youngest ones have gone to bed.

Depend on videos that you already know. One lucky thing about very young children is that they like to watch their favorite videos over and over. There are many wonderful videos that you can buy to have on hand, and there are several newsletters and web sites that review children's videos. You can also tape episodes of good TV programs off the air. When our son was very small, I used to make him tapes of *Sesame Street* and *Mister Rogers' Neighborhood.* What amazed me was how many times he wanted to see the same episodes. For very young children, even these shows are quite complicated, and children seem to enjoy watching them over and over until they become totally familiar with them.

Another tip I've discovered about video viewing is to be certain that your VCR is tuned to a safe channel when your child is viewing a tape. When the tape gets to the end, your television will display whatever channel your VCR is on. If it's PBS or C-SPAN, your child is probably safe. But if it's a major network or a general entertainment cable channel, what your child sees next could be almost anything!

Tape a questionable program and watch it first when your child is not around. If you feel unsure about a program's content despite the ratings systems, previewing it may be the best choice. Also, don't feel that your child has to rush to the theater to see a new movie the first weekend it comes out. By hanging back, you will have much more information at your disposal in making your decision. If you're still not sure, wait for the video. You can screen it first, or at least you can be there when your child sees it. And videos have another advantage: Visual images are not as powerful on the small screen in your well-lit family room as they are on the massive screen of a darkened theater.

And don't forget to be careful about your own TV viewing. Soon after our son was born, we started looking at TV from the perspective of how it would affect our child. What happened first is that we started taping many of our favorite adult-oriented programs for later viewing. But like many other new parents, we found ourselves going to bed earlier and earlier in order to keep up our energy level, and the tapes kept piling up without being viewed. I have gradually come to get less of my entertainment from TV and more from reading, which I can do in the same room as my child without subjecting him to adult fare.

Enlist the cooperation of the parents of your children's friends and the other people who look after your child, including grandparents, baby-sitters, child-care providers, and teachers. Show them this book or tell them about it. Make sure they understand that you're not being silly or overprotective—that your concerns are based on sound research involving data from thousands of children and hundreds of parents. Require child-care providers and schools to obtain parental permission for the showing of entertainment videos.

Don't worry too much. Remember, knowledge is power! The purpose of this book is not to frighten *you!* It's simply to give you better information and tools to guide your child safely through the unpredictable world of television and movies. Just being there and being aware will go a long way toward preventing the types of long-term anxieties and fears we've seen throughout this book. And remember, if your child becomes frightened, there are ways of helping him deal with that fear. If your child stumbles into a disastrous program choice—and that's probably inevitable once in a while—the important thing is to be there for him and help him handle his fears. The fact that you now understand why your child is afraid and know the types of fear-reducing strategies that are most likely to help at your child's age should be greatly reassuring to you and will certainly help you reassure your child.

Making Sure Your Voice Is Heard

Beyond what you can do in your home and for your own family, there are certain steps you can take to help change the television landscape and the media environment we all live in.

First, be sure that your local television station hears your complaints when you think that something inappropriate is on television at a time or in a place that children are likely to be adversely affected by it. During the controversy over the TV ratings, many local stations said they weren't hearing complaints from parents. Perhaps parents had given up, feeling no one was listening to them. If you have time, make your complaint in writing and send a copy to your local paper as a letter to the editor so that other parents may be informed as well. You should also complain when you think a program has been inappropriately rated. Although local stations usually accept the ratings that are provided by the program producers or distributors, they can change ratings that they consider inappropriate. Also, send your complaints to the TV Parental Guidelines Monitoring Board (see the appendix for the address) and the FCC. And be sure that your representatives in Congress know your views. Congress has been extremely responsive to the feelings of parents on this issue.

What we have learned from the controversy over the rating system is that parents do have a voice in these matters, and when the chorus is large, it is heard with resounding clarity. Parents like us can influence how decisions are made in Congress and can force the television industry to be responsive.

There are other things we should be asking the entertainment industry to do to help us protect our children. Here are a few ideas:

Television stations should not air promotional ads for frightening shows and movies during programs with a sizable child audience. Even a promo can cause long-term fears, and parents need more assurance that their child will not be exposed to this type of material when viewing a program that would otherwise be safe.

In general, programmers should agree not to air promos for shows with higher-level ratings in shows with lower ratings. But even if we could get the industry to agree to this, it would not address the fact that many shows are not rated. News and sports, which are not rated, are frequently used to promote other shows. I have received many complaints from parents about the frightening promotions that were aired during recent World Series and Super Bowl telecasts. I realize that one reason networks are willing to pay so much for blockbuster sports events is to promote their other shows. However, networks should be sensitive to the fact that these events are viewed by many children. If a show with controversial content is promoted during a lower-rated or nonrated show, the ad should be designed with a general audience in mind. At the very least, it should exclude the visually frightening elements of the program being promoted.

Movie advertisements and videocassette packages should include the MPAA's reasons for a rating along with the rating. The content that was responsible for the rating a movie received needs to be readily accessible at the time viewing decisions are frequently made—while reading the paper or visiting the video store. And we could really use this type of information for movies rated before 1995. Wouldn't it be helpful if the VCR package for the PG-rated *My Girl* let us know that the movie was about a young girl who is convinced she has contracted a variety of deadly diseases and whose best friend dies from a bee sting? Incidentally, according to the *Motion Picture Rating Directory,* that movie was originally rated PG-13, but the rating was reduced to PG after an appeal.

Family restaurants should not offer toys aimed at preschoolers that tie in with movies that are too scary for that audience. The marketing of *Jurassic Park* was a prime example of a promotional campaign that drew many youngsters to a movie that was clearly too horrifying for them. In an ideal world, the businesspeople making agreements for restaurant tie-ins would show an advance copy of the movie to their own young children before agreeing to promote it to toddlers! But seriously, businesses that cross-promote movies should feel the responsibility to choose the movies they pitch with care.

Let Other People Know When Your Child Has a Negative Emotional Reaction to Something in the Media

This is perhaps the most important thing you can do besides being vigilant about what your children watch. If your child has a fright reaction, you are certainly not alone. Your child is not odd, unstable, or otherwise unbalanced, and there are good reasons why the reaction occurred. Sharing your experience with others will no doubt be therapeutic for you, and it's important to warn other parents about potential effects on their children. If enough parents speak out, we may very well be able to achieve better ratings of programs and movies and more family-friendly programming practices in general.

There are many other changes the entertainment industry could introduce to make television and movies more predictable and less of a minefield for families. Most parents don't want governmental censorship; they don't want adults to be prevented from seeing the adult fare they enjoy. But they do want to protect their children from viewing harmful content—or content they consider inappropriate—without their knowledge in their own homes!

The entertainment industry is extremely well-heeled and its effects are pervasive. But if we communicate with each other and make our needs and wishes known to child advocacy groups, legislators, advertisers, and programmers, we can make the media environment safer for our children. That way, all of us will rest—*and sleep*—easier.

Acknowledgments

I owe so many people so much for helping to make this book a reality that it is difficult to know where to start. But it seems only right that I begin with the person who got me started in research in the first place—Professor Dolf Zillmann of the University of Alabama. It was Dolf who found me as an uncertain first-semester graduate student at the University of Pennsylvania's Annenberg School for Communication and transformed me into an enthusiastic and dedicated researcher. He not only taught me to have high standards as a researcher, but he showed me how much fun and how rewarding the entire research process could be.

Next I want to thank my research collaborators and coauthors who contributed so much to the studies reported here. Special gratitude goes to my first three doctoral advisees, whose contributions during the initial stages of the research were so essential to turning some ideas sketched out in a grant proposal into innovative research procedures and then into influential scholarly publications. To these three most important collaborators, Professor Glenn Sparks (now at Purdue University), Professor Barbara J. Wilson (now at the University of California, Santa Barbara), and Professor Cynthia Hoffner (now at Illinois State University), I owe an enormous debt for assisting me in mapping out the terrain of this program of research. Other important collaborators and coauthors whose work is central to the information and advice given in these pages are Professor Marie-Louise Mares (now at the University of Pennsylvania's Annenberg School for Communication), Professor Mary Beth Oliver (now at Penn. State), Professor Marina Krcmar (now at the University of Connecticut), Dr. Lisa Bruce, and especially Professor Kristen Harrison (now at the University of Michigan) and Dr. Amy Nathanson (now at the University of California, Santa Barbara). I also wish to thank my colleagues at the University of Wisconsin, especially Professor Denise Solomon and Dean Mary Anne Fitzpatrick, for their valuable help and encouragement.

I particularly want to thank Victoria Duran, program director of the National PTA, for her enormous intellectual and moral support of my research on television ratings. Working with her and the leadership of the National PTA has been richly rewarding both personally and professionally, and I have come to appreciate the power of an idealistic and dedicated grassroots organization to affect public policy in a way that benefits America's families.

I have been extremely fortunate to receive the generous financial support that made this research possible. The initial grant from the National Institute of Mental Health was essential to getting my research in this area off the ground. I am also indebted to the University of Wisconsin for generously funding many of these studies and for providing me a supportive work environment for the past two dozen years. Thanks are also due to the Institute for Mental Health Initiatives for helping to fund the parent survey on ratings, to the H. F. Guggenheim Foundation for supporting my research on the attractions of violence, and to the National Cable Television Association for supporting my research on children's reactions to television ratings.

I would also like to thank Linda Henzl for her expert and enthusiastic assistance with the manuscript for this book and so many other projects; Debbie Hanson for her patient handling of all the accounting on my grants; and Paddy Rourke and Dave Fritsch for their generous technical support. I am also very thankful to the many students who helped out in various ways in conducting the research. I am especially indebted to all the children, parents, and college students who participated in my research or told me about their experiences. It is their contributions, after all, that comprise the essence of this book.

I have also benefitted greatly from the encouragement of several people in the fields of communication and mental health, especially Kathryn Montgomery and Jeffrey Chester of the Center for Media Education; Suzanne Stutman of the Institute for Mental Health Initiatives; Ed Donnerstein and Joel Federman of the University of California, Santa Barbara; and Patti Valkenburg of the University of Amsterdam.

With all this support, I still don't know how I would have arrived at a book without the help and guidance of Joan Fischer. It was Joan who helped me get started on this project, collaborating with me on the first proposal for this book, helping me find my own voice as a writer to an audience of parents, and providing valuable support and suggestions all along the way.

I am also deeply indebted to Kate Wendleton, whose advice on getting this book published was crucial; to my agent, Alex Holtz, who immediately made things happen and became a good friend in the process; to Vicki Austin-Smith, my editor at Harcourt Brace, for her unbridled enthusiasm and helpful suggestions; and to Rachel Myers, for her enormously thoughtful and creative copy editing.

Friends and family have also been extremely helpful and supportive, especially my brother Jim Cantor and my sister Mary Hammer, as well as Dorothy Cantor, Sara Larsen, Bonnie Holcomb, and Carol and Jim Lieberman.

Most importantly, I thank the people closest to me: first, my parents, Liz and Chips Cantor, who provided me with a loving home and have always been there when I needed them. Sadly, just as I was completing the manuscript for this book, my mother passed away. Although I miss her enormously, I carry her love and warmth with me every moment, and I am eternally grateful for the ideal role model she has been as a wife, as a mother, and as a woman who contributed her talents and energies for the benefit of the larger community.

And I couldn't have done any of this without my husband, Bob Larsen, and my son, Alex. Bob's love and support fuel everything I accomplish and make life in general so much more rewarding. As for Alex, aside from teaching me, from Day One, the deeper meaning of the words "pride and joy," his presence in my life makes me believe all the more in the critical importance of the work I'm doing.

Problems Frequently Caused by Scary Television and Movies

Immediate Reactions:
- Intense fear
- Crying, clinging, trembling
- Stomach problems (stomach aches, vomiting)

Longer-term Reactions:
- Difficulty sleeping
- Nightmares
- Insistence on sleeping with parents
- Dependence on unusual bedtime rituals
- Refusal to be alone or to be in certain areas of the house
- Refusal to engage in normal activities
- Concern about being hurt or killed
- Unnecessary or unreasonably intense fears
- Long-term aversion to common animals (especially dogs, cats, insects, and spiders)
- Anxiety in specific situations (especially swimming)

The Most Troublesome Content for Different Ages

(Remember, Age Trends Are Approximate)

Two- to Seven-Year-Olds:
- Visual images, whether realistic or fantastic, that are naturally scary: vicious animals; monsters; grotesque, mutilated, or deformed characters
- Physical transformations of characters, especially when a normal character becomes grotesque
- Stories involving the death of a parent
- Stories involving natural disasters, shown vividly

Seven- to Twelve-Year-Olds:
- More realistic threats and dangers that can happen, especially things that can happen to the child
- Violence or the threat of violence
- Stories involving child victims

Age Thirteen and Up:
- Realistic physical harm or threats of intense harm
- Molestation or sexual assault
- Threats from aliens or occult forces

Tips for Helping Frightened Preschoolers

- Remove them from the scary situation.
- Don't belittle or ignore the fear.
- Provide your physical presence, attention, and warmth.
- Try a drink or a snack and a new activity.
- Consider lower doses of the scary image if they want to conquer their fear.
- Go along with reasonable bedtime rituals.
- Recognize the limited effectiveness of logical explanations. (See chapter 8 for adapting them for younger children.)
- Be firm in your resolve to practice prevention.

Tips for Making Explanations Reassuring to Children

For Fantasy Threats:

- For eight-year-olds and over, get them to focus on the impossibility of fantastic happenings.
- For younger children, visually demonstrate the unreal status of fantastic occurrences. (For example, help them apply scary makeup.)

For Real Threats:

- Avoid indicating that a realistic frightening event is possible but unlikely. (Saying "it hardly ever happens" probably won't help.)
- Give them calming, absolute, but limited truthful information. (Saying "It's never happened here" is more likely to succeed.)
- Use their fears as a teachable moment, and offer safety guidelines about how to protect themselves from the threat.
- Talk to them sympathetically about their fears, even when there's nothing particularly reassuring to say.
- Seek professional help if fears are uncontrollable or overpowering.
- Seek your child's cooperation in avoiding future exposure to similar content.

What You Should Know about the Motion Picture Association of America (MPAA) Ratings

     G: General Audiences. All ages admitted.

    PG: Parental Guidance Suggested. Some material may not be suitable for children.

  PG-13: Parents Strongly Cautioned. Some material may be inappropriate for children under 13.

     R: Restricted. Under 17 requires accompanying parent or adult guardian.

  NC-17: No One 17 and Under Admitted.

- MPAA ratings are decided by majority vote of a committee of parents who judge which rating most parents would find suitable.

- MPAA ratings give age guidelines but don't tell about content.

- Content information for recent movies is now available on the MPAA's web site: www.mpaa.org.

- Only 3 percent of movies rated in 1995 and 1996 were rated G; 14 percent were rated PG; 16 percent were rated PG-13; and 67 percent were rated R.

- 26 percent of PG-rated movies had "bad language" only.

- PG-rated movies (such as *Jaws*) produced before 1984 (when PG-13 was introduced) may be surprisingly intense and scary.

- Even G-rated movies, especially animated adventure features, are often too scary for preschoolers.

A Guide to the Amended TV Parental Guidelines

Children's Programs
TV-Y: All Children
TV-Y7: Directed to Older Children
  FV: Fantasy Violence*

*General Programming***
TV-G: General Audience

TV-PG: Parental Guidance Suggested
  V: Moderate Violence
  S: Sexual Situations
  L: Infrequent Coarse Language
  D: Some Suggestive Dialogue

TV-14: Parents Strongly Cautioned
  V: Intense Violence
  S: Intense Sexual Situations
  L: Strong Coarse Language
  D: Intensely Suggestive Dialogue

TV-MA: Mature Audience Only
  V: Graphic Violence
  S: Explicit Sexual Activity
  L: Crude Indecent Language

*Any intense violence in children's programming is labeled "fantasy violence."
**The most intense level of content determines a program's overall rating. Content existing at lower levels is not displayed.

Contacts Regarding TV and Movie Ratings

TV Parental Guidelines Monitoring Board
P. O. Box 14097
Washington, D.C. 20004
E-mail: tvomb@usa.net
web site: www.tvguidelines.org

Classification and Rating Administration
Motion Picture Association of America, Inc.
15503 Ventura Boulevard
Encino, CA 91436-3103
web site: www.mpaa.org

OKTV (Alternative TV Ratings)
c/o Gaffney-Livingstone Consultation Services
59 Griggs Road
Brookline, MA 02146
web site: www.aacap.org (American Academy of Child and
Adolescent Psychiatry)

Federal Communications Commission
1919 M Street, NW
Washington, D.C. 20554
web site: www.fcc.gov/vchip

Notes

....

A note on these notes: I've included these notes to provide support for the claims I am making by directing your attention to my published research and the writings of others on the topic. But the notes are not meant to be exhaustive in the way the references for a scholarly book would be. More extensive references can be found in many of the academic articles I refer to here.

Preface

p. xv "Recent research on the validity of childhood memories": See C. R. Brewin, B. Andrews, and I. H. Gotlib, "Psychopathology and Early Experience: A Reappraisal of Retrospective Reports," *Psychological Bulletin* 113, no. 1 (1993): 82–98.

Introduction: Is Your Home Really Your Castle?

p. 2 "In fact, research now shows that educational television programming viewed at the preschool level can
really improve children's chances for success much
later in life": P. A. Collins, et al., "Effects of Early Childhood Media Use on Academic Achievement" (paper
presented at Society for Research in Child Development Convention, Washington, D.C., April 1997).

Chapter 1: The Suddenly Crowded
Queen-Size Bed

p. 5 and thereafter. All anecdotes presented in this book
are real, but the names, when included, have been
changed. Some of the reports are based on oral interviews. Most of them (those presented in italics) are
from written reports by students or parents and are in
their own words. Some are from research participants;
others are from class papers. Most of these anecdotes
are excerpts of longer descriptions. The only changes
from the writer's own words involve deletions to reduce wordiness, or corrections in grammar, punctua-
tion, or spelling. None of these anecdotes have been
embellished in any way.

p. 8 "I was amazed by the vividness and emotionality with
which they wrote about their experiences": An interesting article in a popular magazine talks about recent

advances in the neurobiology of memory, which may help us understand why traumatic events often produce such indelible memory traces: S. S. Hall, "Our Memories, Our Selves," *New York Times Magazine*, February 15, 1998, 26–33, 49, 56–57.

p. 9 "I'll call this the retrospective study": K. Harrison and J. Cantor, "Tales from the Screen: Long-Term Anxiety Reactions to Frightening Movies" (paper presented at the International Communication Association Convention, Chicago, May 1996).

p. 11 "But they have often said that writing about it and learning why it may have happened helped them work through some of their anxieties": In fact, there is evidence that writing about emotional experiences has a profoundly beneficial effect on both psychological and physical well-being. For an important and highly readable book on this topic, see J. W. Pennebaker, *Opening Up: The Healing Power of Expressing Emotions* (New York: Guilford Press, 1997).

pp. 12–13 "a number of psychologists and psychiatrists have claimed that [fright reactions to television and films] may cause children to be plagued by nightmares, sleep disturbances, and bizarre fantasies": for example, J. L. Singer, *Daydreaming and Fantasy* (London: Allen & Unwin, 1975); E. P. Sarafino, *The Fears of Childhood: A Guide to Recognizing and Reducing Fearful States* (New York: Human Sciences Press, 1986).

p. 13 "young people who had to be hospitalized for several days or weeks after watching horror movies such as *The Exorcist* and *Invasion of the Body Snatchers*": J. C. Buzzuto, "Cinematic Neurosis Following *The Exorcist*," *Journal of Nervous and Mental Disease* 161 (1975): 43–48; J. Mathai, "An Acute Anxiety State in an Adolescent Precipitated by Viewing a Horror Movie," *Journal of Adolescence* 6 (1983): 197–200.

p. 13 "two children had suffered from post-traumatic stress disorder": D. Simons and W. R. Silveira, "Post-traumatic Stress Disorder in Children after Television Programmes," *British Medical Journal* 308 (1994): 389–90.

p. 19 "Many of the symptoms . . . are well-known symptoms of both phobias and post-traumatic stress disorder": See "Specific Phobias" and "Post-Traumatic Stress Disorder" in *Diagnostic and Statistical Manual of Mental Disorders,* 4th ed. (Washington, D.C.: American Psychiatric Association, 1994).

p. 20 "my colleagues and I designed a study to observe [spillover effects]": J. Cantor and B. Omdahl, "Effects of Fictional Media Depictions of Realistic Threats on Children's Emotional Responses, Expectations, Worries, and Liking for Related Activities," *Communication Monographs* 58 (1991): 384–401.

p. 20 "*Little House on the Prairie* . . . was among the top-ten fear-producing shows according to a survey of parents my collaborators and I conducted in the early eighties":

J. Cantor and G. G. Sparks, "Children's Fear Responses to Mass Media: Testing Some Piagetian Predictions," *Journal of Communication* 34, no. 2 (1984): 90–103.

p. 23 *"After this incident, I would not go down into our basement":* In a study of the media-induced fright of college students, 10% of males and 68% of females agreed with the statement, "I have sometimes been SO scared of a show or movie that I have actually been afraid to go into certain rooms in my own house." G. G. Sparks, M. M. Spirek, and K. Hodgson, "Individual Differences in Arousability: Implications for Understanding Immediate and Lingering Emotional Reactions to Frightening Mass Media," *Communication Quarterly* 41, no. 4 (1993): 465–76.

p. 25 "To explore more systematically what parents know . . . my colleagues and I recently conducted a phone survey": Some of these findings are reported in J. Cantor and A. Nathanson, "Children's Fright Reactions to Television News," *Journal of Communication* 46, no. 4 (1996): 139–52.

Chapter 2: Through a Child's Eyes

p. 33 "Our retrospective study of college students showed that more than half of those who reported a long-term fright reaction had not particularly wanted to see the program that had caused them to be so upset": K. Harrison and J. Cantor, "Tales from the Screen: Long-Term Anxiety Reactions to Frightening Movies" (paper presented at the International Communication Association Convention, Chicago, May 1996).

p. 39 "Some well-known psychoanalysts have proposed that these stories allow children to work through 'traumas that are seething in the unconscious'": For example, B. Bettelheim, *The Uses of Enchantment: The Meaning and Importance of Fairy Tales* (New York: Vintage Books, 1975).

Chapter 3: Appearance, Appearance, Appearance

p. 50 "Research shows that very young children respond to things mainly in terms of how they appear": See, for example, R. Melkman, B. Tversky, and D. Baratz, "Developmental Trends in the Use of Perceptual and Conceptual Attributes in Grouping, Clustering, and Retrieval," *Journal of Experimental Child Psychology* 31 (1981): 470–86.

p. 51 "A follower of Piaget noted that young children focus on and react to whatever 'clamors loudest for their attention'": J. Flavell, *The Developmental Psychology of Jean Piaget* (New York: Van Nostrand, 1963).

p. 52 "The first thing my colleagues and I did to explore this idea was to ask parents which programs and movies had frightened their children the most": J. Cantor and G. G. Sparks, "Children's Fear Responses to Mass Media: Testing Some Piagetian Predictions," *Journal of Communication* 34, no. 2 (1984): 90–103.

p. 55 "my colleagues and I answered the question about

how sensitive to appearance different age groups are by doing a controlled experiment": C. Hoffner and J. Cantor, "Developmental Differences in Responses to a Television Character's Appearance and Behavior," *Developmental Psychology* 21 (1985): 1065–74.

p. 58 "In the survey we conducted in the early eighties, [*The Amityville Horror*] was reported to have scared many more older children than younger ones": J. Cantor and G. G. Sparks, "Children's Fear Responses to Mass Media: Testing Some Piagetian Predictions," *Journal of Communication* 34, no. 2 (1984): 90–103.

p. 59 "When we conducted a random phone survey of parents the night after [*The Day After*] aired": J. Cantor, B. J. Wilson, and C. Hoffner, "Emotional Responses to a Televised Nuclear Holocaust Film," *Communication Research* 13 (1986): 257–77.

p. 64 "Certain types of animals, especially snakes and spiders, more readily evoke fear than other types": See G. S. Hall, "A Study of Fear," *The American Journal of Psychology* 9, no. 2 (1897): 147–249; A. Maurer, "What Children Fear," *The Journal of Genetic Psychology* 106 (1965): 265–77; D. R. Kirkpatrick, "Age, Gender and Patterns of Common Intense Fears Among Adults," *Behavior Research and Therapy* 22, no. 2 (1984): 141–50; R. M. Yerkes and A. W. Yerkes, "Nature and Condition of Avoidance (Fear) in Chimpanzee," *Journal of Comparative Psychology* 21 (1936): 53–66.

p. 64 "A third type of visual image that automatically repels and scares us is physical deformity": See D. O. Hebb, "On the Nature of Fear," *Psychological Review* 53 (1946): 259–76.

p. 66 "Researchers have identified a small part of the brain called the amygdala as the center where innately threatening sights and sounds are received": See J. LeDoux, *The Emotional Brain: The Mysterious Underpinnings of Emotional Life* (New York: Simon & Schuster, 1996); R. J. Davidson and S. K. Sutton, "Affective Neuroscience: The Emergence of a Discipline," *Current Opinion in Neurobiology* 5 (1995): 217–24; R. J. Davidson, "Affective Style and Affective Disorders: Perspectives from Affective Neuroscience," *Cognition and Emotion* (1998, in press).

Chapter 4: The Trouble with Transformations

p. 72 "by Piaget's descriptions of how children . . . respond": For a reader-friendly introduction to Piaget, see D. G. Singer and T. A. Revenson, *A Piaget Primer: How a Child Thinks* (New York: Plume, 1996). For a more comprehensive treatment of Piaget's major theoretical principles, see J. Flavell, *The Developmental Psychology of Jean Piaget* (New York: Van Nostrand, 1963).

p. 74 "I soon discovered how frightening young children found [*The Incredible Hulk*] when I looked at the results of the parent survey we conducted in the spring

of 1981": J. Cantor and G. G. Sparks, "Children's Fear
Responses to Mass Media: Testing Some Piagetian Predictions," *Journal of Communication* 34 no. 2 (1984):
90–103.

p. 75 "After finding that young children did indeed find
[*The Incredible Hulk*] scary, at least according to their
parents, we designed a study to learn more about the
reasons for this reaction": G. G. Sparks and J. Cantor,
"Developmental Differences in Fright Responses to a
Television Program Depicting a Character Transformation," *Journal of Broadcasting & Electronic Media* 30
(1986): 309–23.

p. 82 "in one famous study, children between the ages of
three and six were allowed to pet a tame and friendly
cat": R. DeVries, *Constancy of Generic Identity in the Years
Three to Six*, Monographs of the Society for Research
in Child Development, serial no. 127, vol. 34, no. 3
(Chicago: University of Chicago Press for the Society
for Research in Child Development, 1969).

Chapter 5: "But It's Only Make-Believe"

pp. 89–90 "Developmental psychologists have noted that
children only gradually come to understand the difference between reality and fantasy": For example, P.
Morison and H. Gardner, "Dragons and Dinosaurs:
The Child's Capacity to Differentiate Fantasy from Reality," *Child Development* 49 (1978): 642–48.

p. 91 "Piaget's take on this situation was to say that pre-school, or preoperational, children do not distinguish play and reality as two distinct realms with different ground rules": J. Flavell, *The Developmental Psychology of Jean Piaget* (New York: Van Nostrand, 1963).

pp. 92–93 "At first children believe that the things they are seeing are actually inside the television set—that if they look inside, they'll find those things and that what's in there might actually be able to come out": J. H. Flavell, et al., "Do Young Children Think of Television Images as Pictures or Real Objects?" *Journal of Broadcasting & Electronic Media* 34, no. 4 (1990): 399–419.

p. 93 "They come to judge whether something on television is real on the basis of whether the things they see in a story actually exist in the real world": P. Morison, H. Kelly, and H. Gardner, "Reasoning about the Realities on Television: A Developmental Study." *Journal of Broadcasting & Electronic Media* 25, no. 3 (1981): 229–41.

p. 95 "In the survey we conducted in the early eighties . . . we categorized the content as either fantasy or fiction": J. Cantor and G. G. Sparks, "Children's Fear Responses to Mass Media: Testing Some Piagetian Predictions," *Journal of Communication* 34 no. 2 (1984): 90–103.

p. 95 "Our more recent survey of parents of children in kindergarten, second, fourth, and sixth grade recon-firmed the importance of the fantasy-reality distinc-tion in what frightens children": Some of these findings are reported in J. Cantor and A. Nathanson, "Children's Fright Reactions to Television News," *Journal of Communication* 46, no. 4 (1996): 139–52.

p. 98 "There are several reasons why we respond so intensely to television shows and movies, even when we know that what we're seeing is fiction": For more discussion of these ideas, see J. Cantor, "Fright Reactions to Mass Media," in *Media Effects: Advances in Theory and Research,* ed. by J. Bryant and D. Zillmann (Hillsdale, N.J.: Erlbaum, 1994): 213–45.

p. 102 "Most scary programs and movies let us know what is going to happen or what might happen, and we become anxious well in advance of the horrifying outcome. Research shows that it's much more frightening this way": J. Cantor, D. Ziemke, and G. G. Sparks, "The Effect of Forewarning on Emotional Responses to a Horror Film," *Journal of Broadcasting* 28 (1984): 21–31; C. Hoffner and J. Cantor, "Forewarning of Threat and Prior Knowledge of Outcome: Effects on Children's Emotional Responses to a Film Sequence," *Human Communication Research* 16 (1990): 323–54.

p. 102 "It seems that music and sound effects dramatically affect our emotional reactions": There is surprisingly little controlled research that supports this claim. One study showed that different musical scores increased or reduced physiological responses to a stressful film but did not affect viewers' ratings of their feelings of anxiety: J. F. Thayer and R. W. Levenson, "Effects of

Music on Psychophysiological Responses to a Stressful Film," *Psychomusicology* 3, no. 1 (1983): 44–52. Another study reported that of three animated cartoons, the one that produced the most anxiety in children was the one that had no violence but had the most "fear-eliciting sound effects": K. Björkqvist and K. Lagerspetz, "Children's Experience of Three Types of Cartoon at Two Age Levels," *International Journal of Psychology* 20 (1985): 77–93. More research is needed on the power of music and sound effects.

p. 104 "Content analyses have shown that in horror movies, attacks against men are usually over and done with quickly, but attacks against women are longer and more drawn out": F. Molitor and B. S. Sapolsky, "Sex, Violence, and Victimization in Slasher Films," *Journal of Broadcasting & Electronic Media* 37, no. 2 (1993): 233–42.

Chapter 6: When Reality Is a Nightmare

p. 112 "A recent study reported that local news is especially violent": "Body Bag Journalism," *Sacramento Bee,* May 22, 1997, sec. B, p. 6.

p. 112 "In the survey we did in the early eighties, in which we asked parents to name the television shows and movies that had frightened their child, television news stories were in the top ten": J. Cantor and G. G. Sparks, "Children's Fear Responses to Mass Media: Testing Some Piagetian Predictions," *Journal of Communication* 34 no. 2 (1984): 90–103.

p. 113 "shortly after the war in the Persian Gulf, almost half of a random sample of parents my colleagues and I contacted said their child had been upset by television coverage of the war": J. Cantor, M. L. Mares, and M. B. Oliver, "Parents' and Children's Emotional Reactions to Televised Coverage of the Gulf War," in *Desert Storm and the Mass Media,* ed. by B. Greenberg and W. Gantz (Cresskill, N.J.: Hampton Press, 1993): 325–40.

p. 113 "in the random survey of parents with children in kindergarten through sixth grade that we did in the spring of 1994, we found that 37 percent said their child had been frightened or upset by a television news story during the preceding year": J. Cantor and A. Nathanson, "Children's Fright Reactions to Television News," *Journal of Communication* 46, no. 4 (1996): 139–52.

p. 115 "Dozens of studies have been conducted in which children have been asked what frightens them, and there is a large consensus regarding age trends in fears": For a review, see J. Cantor, B. J. Wilson, and C. Hoffner, "Emotional Responses to a Televised Nuclear Holocaust Film," *Communication Research* 13 (1986): 257–77.

p. 119 "In our most recent random survey of parents, *Rescue 911* was mentioned more often than any other program (including fantasy and fiction genres) as causing fear in children": Other findings from this survey are reported in J. Cantor and A. Nathanson, "Children's Fright Reactions to Television News," *Journal of Communication* 46, no. 4 (1996): 139–52.

Chapter 7: When Words Won't Work

p. 125 "An early study of children and fear tells the story of the young child who sat down and classified fairy-tale characters as 'real' or 'unreal' ": A. T. Jersild and F. B. Holmes, "Methods of Overcoming Children's Fears," *Journal of Psychology* 1 (1935): 75–104.

p. 125 "When my colleagues and I questioned parents of preschoolers in a survey, most of them said they used that type of explanation when coping with their child's TV fears": B. J. Wilson and J. Cantor, "Reducing Children's Fear Reactions to Mass Media: Effects of Visual Exposure and Verbal Explanation," in *Communication Yearbook 10* (Beverly Hills, Calif.: Sage, 1987): 553–73.

p. 125 "We took a scene from *The Wizard of Oz* that many children find especially scary": J. Cantor and B. J. Wilson, "Modifying Fear Responses to Mass Media in Preschool and Elementary School Children," *Journal of Broadcasting* 28 (1984): 431–43.

p. 126 "When my colleagues and I asked children to indicate how helpful different methods would be in making them feel better if they were scared by something on TV": B. J. Wilson, C. Hoffner, and J. Cantor, "Children's Perceptions of the Effectiveness of Techniques to Reduce Fear from Mass Media," *Journal of Applied Developmental Psychology* 8 (1987): 39–52.

p. 127 "Another experiment my colleagues and I conducted is a case in point. The results surprised us": B. J. Wilson and J. Cantor, "Reducing Children's Fear

Reactions to Mass Media: Effects of Visual Exposure and Verbal Explanation," in *Communication Yearbook 10* (Beverly Hills, Calif.: Sage, 1987): 553–73.

p. 129 "The same preschoolers . . . said that getting something to eat or drink or holding a blanket or cuddly toy would help them the most": B. J. Wilson, C. Hoffner, and J. Cantor, "Children's Perceptions of the Effectiveness of Techniques to Reduce Fear from Mass Media," *Journal of Applied Developmental Psychology* 8 (1987): 39–52.

p. 129 "An interesting experiment was recently reported in which preschoolers watched a scary television movie with or without their older sister or brother": B. J. Wilson and A. J. Weiss, "The Effects of Sibling Coviewing on Preschoolers' Reactions to a Suspenseful Movie Scene," *Communication Research* 20, no. 2 (1993): 214–48.

p. 132 "Experts differ, sometimes vehemently, on whether [sleeping in a parent's bed] should ever be allowed": Rather than jumping into this controversy, I'll direct you to some differing opinions on the subject: R. Ferber, *Solve Your Child's Sleep Problems* (New York: Simon & Schuster, 1985). This book argues against letting your child sleep with you and has many thoughtful recommendations regarding how to handle children's nighttime fears. R. Wright, "Go Ahead . . . Sleep with Your Children," *APA Monitor* (American Psychological Association) (June 1997): 16. (Also published in *Slate*, www.

slate.com/Code/Reg3/Login.asp?ur/path-Earthling/ 97-03-27/Earthling.asp). Wright proposes, using arguments from evolutionary theory, that "the family bed" is superior to having your baby sleep alone. Both Penelope Leach and T. Berry Brazelton steer a middle ground, and present the benefits and drawbacks of both approaches: P. Leach, *Your Baby and Child: From Birth to Age Five* (New York: Alfred A. Knopf, 1990); T. B. Brazelton, *Touchpoints: Your Child's Emotional and Behavioral Development* (Reading, Mass.: Addison-Wesley, 1992).

p. 135 "exposing themselves to bits and pieces of the program rather than the whole thing. Research shows that these techniques can actually reduce younger children's fright while viewing scary programs": B. J. Wilson, "The Effects of Two Control Strategies on Children's Emotional Reactions to a Frightening Movie Scene," *Journal of Broadcasting & Electronic Media* 33 (1989): 397–418.

p. 135 "In the experiment we did with *Raiders of the Lost Ark* we also explored whether we could make the snake scene less frightening by desensitizing children to the visual image of snakes": B. J. Wilson and J. Cantor, "Reducing Children's Fear Reactions to Mass Media: Effects of Visual Exposure and Verbal Explanation," in *Communication Yearbook 10* (Beverly Hills, Calif.: Sage, 1987): 553–73.

p. 136 "Other researchers have found similar results by allowing children to hold rubber replicas of spiders or showing them real lizards and worms before they saw scary movies involving these creatures": B. J. Wilson, "Reducing Children's Emotional Reactions to Mass Media Through Rehearsed Explanation and Exposure to a Replica of a Fear Object," *Human Communication Research* 14 (1987): 3–26; B. J. Wilson, "Desensitizing Children's Emotional Reactions to the Mass Media," *Communication Research* 16 (1989): 723–45; A. J. Weiss, D. L. Imrich, and B. J. Wilson, "Prior Exposure to Creatures from a Horror Film: Live Versus Photographic Representation," *Human Communication Research* 20 (1993): 41–66.

p. 136 "My colleagues and I have also taken on *The Incredible Hulk,* using segments of a *Mister Rogers' Neighborhood* episode intended to reduce children's fear of the Hulk": J. Cantor, G. G. Sparks, and C. Hoffner, "Calming Children's Television Fears: Mr. Rogers vs. the Incredible Hulk," *Journal of Broadcasting & Electronic Media* 32 (1988): 271–88.

Chapter 8: Making Explanations Child-Friendly

p. 142 "In the *Wizard of Oz* study, nine- to eleven-year-olds who were told to remember that the witch was not real showed less fear while watching her in a scene": J. Cantor and B. J. Wilson, "Modifying Fear Responses to Mass Media in Preschool and Elementary School Children," *Journal of Broadcasting* 28 (1984): 431–43.

pp. 142–43 "Similarly, other researchers have reported

that seven- to nine-year-olds had their vampire-movie fears reduced by an explanation of how makeup made the vampires look scary, while five- to six-year-olds were not helped": B. J. Wilson and A. J. Weiss, "The effects of two reality explanations on children's reactions to a frightening movie scene," *Communication Monographs* 58 (1991): 307–26.

p. 143 "in a study involving *The Incredible Hulk*, my colleagues and I tried to counteract children's fears by giving them simple explanations of how the Hulk likes to help people, while showing them footage": J. Cantor, G. G. Sparks, and C. Hoffner, "Calming Children's Television Fears: Mr. Rogers vs. the Incredible Hulk," *Journal of Broadcasting & Electronic Media* 32 (1988): 271–88.

p. 143 "For that study, in which we used a scene from the sci-fi thriller *The Blob*, we tried to reassure children by describing the special effects that made the blob look real and letting them create their own 'blobs' out of gelatin and food coloring": J. Cantor and C. Hoffner, "Children's Fear Reactions to a Televised Film as a Function of Perceived Immediacy of Depicted Threat," *Journal of Broadcasting & Electronic Media* 34, no. 4 (1990): 421–42. This technique was used after the study was over, to ensure that children did not leave the experiment with residual feelings of anxiety. Because there was no control condition that did not receive this treatment, we did not collect data to support the treatment's effectiveness as a fear reducer.

pp. 145–46 "In the study involving *The Blob*...we explained to a group of five- to eight-year-olds that a
frightening event in a movie could *never* happen anywhere": J. Cantor and C. Hoffner, "Children's Fear Reactions to a Televised Film as a Function of Perceived
Immediacy of Depicted Threat," *Journal of Broadcasting & Electronic Media* 34 (1990): 421–42.

p. 146 "This finding is consistent with research my colleagues and I have done on children's understanding
of concepts related to probability and likelihood":
D. M. Badzinski, J. Cantor, and C. Hoffner, "Children's
Understanding of Quantifiers," *Child Study Journal* 19
(1989): 241–58; C. Hoffner, J. Cantor, and D. M.
Badzinski, "Children's Understanding of Adverbs De-
noting Degree of Likelihood," *Journal of Child Language* 17 (1990): 217–31.

p. 146 "However, research indicates that older children
and even adults also overestimate the likelihood of
outcomes that are intensely threatening, even when
the chances of their happening are infinitesimal": See
P. Slovic, B. Fischhoff, and S. Lichtenstein, "Facts versus Fears: Understanding Perceived Risk," in *Judgment
under Uncertainty: Heuristics and Biases,* ed. by D. Kah-
neman, P. Slovic, and A. Tversky (Cambridge: Cambridge University Press, 1982).

p. 150 "In the study I reported in chapter 1, in which we
showed the schoolhouse burn down in *Little House on
the Prairie,* we ended the session by giving children

basic fire-safety guidelines": J. Cantor and B. Omdahl, "Effects of Fictional Media Depictions of Realistic Threats on Children's Emotional Responses, Expectations, Worries, and Liking for Related Activities," *Communication Monographs* 58 (1991): 384–401.

p. 155 "In fact, I never did make that appointment with the therapist": Some interesting research in interpersonal communication suggests that when you think about a problem with the intention of talking about it, your thoughts become better suited to solving the problem, whether you ultimately have a conversation about it or not. See D. H. Cloven and M. E. Roloff, "Sense-Making Activities and Interpersonal Conflict, II: The Effects of Communicative Intentions on Internal Dialogue," *Western Journal of Communication* 57 (1993): 309–29. By simply thinking about what I would say to a therapist, I was apparently able to put the problem in a more reasonable perspective.

Chapter 9: Why Kids Are Drawn to Scary Entertainment

Many of the ideas in this chapter are distilled from J. Cantor, "Children's Attraction to Violent Television Programming," in *Why We Watch: The Attractions of Violent Entertainment,* ed. by J. Goldstein (New York: Oxford University Press, 1998).

p. 158 "Nielsen ratings consistently show that most of the Saturday-morning programs with the highest child viewership are violent": For example, H. Stipp, "Children's Viewing of News, Reality-Shows, and Other Programming" (paper presented at the Convention of the International Communication Association, Albuquerque, N.M., May 1995).

p. 159 "A second reason we have so many violent programs and movies is that it is more profitable to produce shows that can be exported to foreign countries": S. Stossel, "The Man Who Counts the Killings," *The Atlantic Monthly* 279, no. 5 (1997): 86–104. This claim is attributed to media researcher and activist George Gerbner. The article chronicles Dr. Gerbner's research on the content of television over the past 30 years. Gerbner contends, as I do, that television viewing promotes feelings of anxiety. His work has a different emphasis from mine: He focuses on the cumulative effects of exposure to violent programming on our perceptions of the world as a mean and dangerous place, rather than on the emotional impact of a single frightening program or movie.

p. 161 "when a researcher asked sixth- to eighth-grade children in Milwaukee the question: 'Would you watch a television program if you knew it contained a lot of violence?' 82 percent replied 'yes' ": L. Bruce, "At the Intersection of Real-Life and Television Violence: Emotional Effects, Cognitive Effects, and Interpretive Activities of Children" (PH.D. diss., University of Wisconsin, Madison, 1995).

p. 163 "Some researchers have even argued that it is action (characters moving fast) rather than violence (characters injuring each other) that attracts children's attention to violent television programs": R. Potts, A. Huston, and J. C. Wright, "The Effects of Television Form and Violent Content on Boys' Attention and Social Behavior," *Journal of Experimental Child Psychology* 41 (1986): 1–17.

p. 163 "Many people, and children especially, enjoy violent, scary shows because they like the thrill of being stimulated and aroused by entertainment": For an interesting analysis of the role of arousal in media entertainment, see D. Zillmann, "Television Viewing and Physiological Arousal," in *Responding to the Screen: Reception and Reaction Processes,* ed. by J. Bryant and D. Zillmann (Hillsdale, N.J.: Erlbaum, 1991): 103–33.

p. 164 "Some psychologists believe that this difference is due to the fact that we treat our little boys differently from our little girls": A. Frodi, J. Macaulay, and P. Thome, "Are Women Always Less Aggressive Than Men? A Review of the Experimental Literature," *Psychological Bulletin* 84 (1977): 634–60.

p. 164 "Other psychologists maintain that boys' greater interest in violence is rooted in their hormones, and that biology predisposes them to be more aggressive and to be more interested in aggressive things": J. Goldstein, "Immortal Kombat: War Toys and Violent Videogames," in *Why We Watch: The Attractions of Violent*

Entertainment, ed. by J. Goldstein (New York: Oxford University Press, 1998).

pp. 164–65 "It has also been shown that children who are more violent themselves are more interested in viewing violent programs": For example, C. Atkin, et al., "Selective Exposure to Televised Violence," *Journal of Broadcasting* 23, no. 1 (1979): 5–13.

p. 165 "Viewing violence contributes to children becoming more violent, and children who are violent are more interested in viewing violence": See L. R. Huesmann, "Psychological Processes Promoting the Relation between Exposure to Media Violence and Aggressive Behavior by the Viewer," *Journal of Social Issues* 42, no. 3 (1986): 125–40.

p. 166 "In one study, college students took a six-weeks' heavy dose of action-adventure programs featuring good triumphing over evil": J. Bryant, R. A. Carveth, and D. Brown, "Television Viewing and Anxiety: An Experimental Examination," *Journal of Communication* 31, no. 1 (1981): 106–19.

p. 166 "In one survey of parents, for example, we found that children who had been frightened by television were especially interested in violent programs in which good triumphed over evil": J. Cantor and A. Nathanson, "Predictors of Children's Interest in Violent Television Programming," *Journal of Broadcasting & Electronic Media* 41 (1997): 155–67.

p. 168 "In a study of children in inner-city Milwaukee": L.

Bruce, "At the Intersection of Real-Life and Television Violence: Emotional Effects, Cognitive Effects, and Interpretive Activities of Children" (Ph.D. diss., University of Wisconsin, Madison, 1995).

p. 169 "Research shows that children who watch a lot of violence become less aroused by it over time and that children become less bothered by real interpersonal aggression after watching fictionalized violence": V. B. Cline, R. G. Croft, and S. Courrier, "Desensitization of Children to Television Violence," *Journal of Personality and Social Psychology* 27, no. 3 (1973): 360–65; F. Molitor and K. W. Hirsch, "Children's Toleration of Real-life Aggression after Exposure to Media Violence: a Replication of the Drabman and Thomas Studies," *Child Study Journal* 24, no. 3 (1994): 191–207.

p. 169 "Research also shows that repeated exposure to violence leads to less sympathy for its victims and to the adoption of violent attitudes and behaviors": D. G. Linz, E. Donnerstein, and S. Penrod, "Effects of long-term exposure to violent and sexually degrading depictions of women," *Journal of Personality and Social Psychology* 55 (1988): 758–68; C. R. Mullin and D. Linz, "Desensitization and Resensitization to Violence Against Women: Effects of Exposure to Sexually Violent Films on Judgments of Domestic Violence Victims," *Journal of Personality and Social Psychology* 69 (1995): 449–59; L. R. Huesmann, "Psychological Processes Promoting the Relation Between Exposure to Media Violence and Aggressive Behavior by the Viewer," *Journal of Social Issues* 42, no. 3 (1986): 125–40.

Chapter 10: Ratings Roulette

p. 172 *"We told our son":* Unlike all the other vignettes that are presented in italics in this book, this anecdote is not a verbatim transcription. It is my re-creation of the story a woman told me when I addressed a group of parents at a local church.

pp. 175–76 "my colleagues and I found that more than one-fourth of [PG-rated movies] had bad language only": J. Cantor, A. Nathanson, and L. L. Henzl, "Reasons Why Movies Received a PG Rating: 1995–1996," Unpublished Report Filed in Comments of Joanne Cantor to the Federal Communications Commission (CS Docket No. 97-55), April 7, 1997.

p. 176 "When my colleagues and I looked at the content of a random sample of movies shown on television, there was only a whisper of a difference between movies rated PG and those rated PG-13": J. Cantor, K. S. Harrison, and M. Krcmar, "Ratings and Advisories: Implications for the New Rating System for Television," in *Television Violence and Public Policy,* ed. by J. T. Hamilton (Ann Arbor: University of Michigan Press, 1998).

p. 177 "one mother who answered a recent nationwide survey of ours": J. Cantor, S. Stutman, and V. Duran, "What Parents Want in a Television Rating System: Results of a National Survey," report released on Capitol

Hill (November 21, 1996), available at www.pta.org/
programs/tvrpttoc.htm.

p. 177 "the explanation of the rating supplied by MPAA
president Jack Valenti hedges a bit": The excerpt
comes from J. Federman, *Media Ratings: Design, Use,
and Consequences* (Studio City, Calif.: Mediascope,
1996). This book gives an excellent review of the use
of media ratings around the world.

p. 178 "In a story in the *Boston Globe,* one mother complained that the wolves in [*Beauty and the Beast*] had
caused her three-year-old daughter to become terrified of dogs": B. F. Meltz, "The Sometimes Terrifying
World of Disney," *Boston Globe*, February 20, 1997, sec.
F., pp. 1, 5. The woman, Jacquie Sears, who also reported that her daughter started worrying that her
parents would die after seeing *Bambi,* has founded
"Mothers Offended by the Media" (MOM), and has
been crusading for better movie ratings ever since.

pp. 183–84 "I joined with the National PTA and the Institute for Mental Health Initiatives (IMHI) to do a nationwide survey to find out what parents wanted in a
rating system": J. Cantor, S. Stutman, and V. Duran,
"What Parents Want in a Television Rating System: Results of a National Survey," report released on Capitol
Hill (November 21, 1996), available at www.pta.org/
programs/tvrpttoc.htm.

p. 186 "This spontaneous comment came from a ten-year-
old girl who participated in research my colleagues

and I conducted for the National Television Violence Study": M. Krcmar and J. Cantor, "The Role of Television Advisories and Ratings in Parent-Child Discussion of Television Viewing Choices," *Journal of Broadcasting & Electronic Media* 41 (1997): 393–411.

p. 187 "My colleagues and I also did some studies to find out how these ratings affect kids who make viewing decisions in the absence of their parents": J. Cantor, K. S. Harrison, and A. Nathanson, "Ratings and Advisories for Television Programming," in *National Television Violence Study*, vol. 2, ed. by Center for Communication and Social Policy, University of California, Santa Barbara (Thousand Oaks, Calif.: Sage Publications, 1997): 267–322.

p. 189 "Jack Valenti had warned critics that he'd see them in court 'in a nanosecond' if they tried to force any changes": G. Browning, "No Oscar for Jack," *National Journal* (August 23, 1997): 1688–91.

Chapter 11: Taming the Resident Monster

p. 195 "Many studies show that viewing more than one or two hours of television a day interferes with a child's other activities": For an interesting review of the literature on this topic, see T. M. MacBeth, "Indirect Effects of Television: Creativity, Persistence, School Achievement, and Participation in Other Activities," in *Tuning in to Young Viewers: Social Science Perspectives* on *Television,* ed. by T. M. MacBeth (Thousand Oaks, Calif.: Sage Publications, 1996): 149–219.

p. 196 "Our research on TV ratings and advisories showed that children whose parents watch TV with them and discuss it with them are less likely to choose restricted content when their parents are not around": These results come from the National Television Violence Study. J. Cantor and K. S. Harrison, "Ratings and Advisories for Television Programming," in *National Television Violence Study,* vol. 1 (Thousand Oaks, Calif.: Sage Publications, 1996): 361–410; J. Cantor, K. S. Harrison, and A. I. Nathanson, "Ratings and Advisories for Television Programming," in *National Television Violence Study,* vol. 2, ed. by Center for Communication and Social Policy, University of California, Santa Barbara (Thousand Oaks, Calif.: Sage Publications, 1997): 267–322.

p. 197 "Research also shows that many parents are concerned about their children's exposure to sexual dialogue, sexual situations, and coarse language, and that parents differ in terms of how strongly they worry about the effects of different types of content": See the parent survey I did with the National PTA and IMHI: J. Cantor, S. Stutman, and V. Duran, "What Parents Want in a Television Rating System: Results of a National Survey," report released on Capitol Hill (November 21, 1996), available at www.pta.org/programs/tvrpttoc.htm.